POOL WARS
On the road to Hell and back
With the world's greatest money players

by Jay Helfert

"Toupee Jay"

iUniverse, Inc.

Bloomington

POOL WARS
On the road to Hell and back
With the world's greatest money players

iUniverse books may be ordered through booksellers or by contacting:

iUniverse
1663 Liberty Drive
Bloomington, IN 47403
www.iuniverse.com
1-800-Authors (1-800-288-4677)

Sleeve Design & Cover Photography © David Thomson Medium Pool

ISBN: 978-1-4759-2591-3 (sc)
ISBN: 978-1-4759-2590-6 (hc)
ISBN: 978-1-4759-2592-0 (e)

Library of Congress Control Number: 2012910099

Printed in the United States of America

iUniverse rev. date: 05/04/2012

Toupee Jay sans toupee

For Dylan and Karly,

So you know a little bit more about your Papa

FOREWORD

Jay Helfert is and has been successful as a pool player, a road warrior, a card player, a stake horse, a gambler, a pool room owner, an entrepreneur, a tournament director, a television commentator, a consultant for film and television as well as a promoter and producer of major professional tournaments. In the pool world, he has been one very busy man.

Don't expect for these stories to be sugar-coated because they are an exact accounting of Jay's genuine experiences, and he brings you to each of them up close and personal. As a seasoned veteran of the pool world, the experiences Jay shares here will keep you on the edge of your seat from the first page to the last.

If you want to see the chronology and evolution of a person who lived and breathed pool as most of us have only dared dream, you'll want to read this book from cover to cover. Pool Wars encompasses forty years of pool history and Jay's 'tell it like it is' style will have you rooted to your chair.

You will feel as if you're there with him, fading the harrowing experiences, making the bets, winning and losing, learning from the con men of long ago. It's the never ending excitement of one realistic experience after another.

Pool Wars is sure to stimulate and rekindle pool players' desire to seek the thrilling excitement shared by Jay chapter after chapter. Now sit back, relax and enjoy Pool Wars.

Joey Aguzin

WELCOME

My wish is that pool fans the world over will enjoy reading this book as much as I enjoyed writing it. It is truly a labor of love, for a game and for its players. I wouldn't trade my years in Pool for anything. I have priceless memories, many of which I now share with you here.

I would like to thank some people who made a difference in my life. My mother and father who taught me right from wrong; my daughter Heather who taught me how to love unconditionally; my son-in-law Aaron who accepted a *rounder* for a father-in-law; my sister Carole and her husband Audie who taught me the value of family and my brother Bruce, the best man I ever knew.

I also wish to thank those who helped me along the way in the pool world. Conrad Burkman who thought enough of my primitive writing to publish it; Mike Panozzo, Mason King, Harold and Shari Stauch, Paul Frankel and JR Calvert who continued to support my writing endeavors; Pat Fleming and Joe Kerr who taught me what being a good tournament director was all about and Ming Ng who helped make the Los Angeles Billiard Expos a reality.

Some of the people who inspired me to write this tome include Walter Tevis who was the greatest writer of them all, Bob Byrne, R.A. Dyer, JD Dolan, Mike Geffner, John Stravinsky, Jon Wertheim and Jeri Engh; all far superior wordsmiths to me.

A special thank you to Joey Aguzin a man of many talents, with pool being only one of them; Freddie "The Beard" Bentivegna who steered me right on this my maiden voyage; Phil Capelle who has been there and done that in the self publishing biz; Ron Bryant for all his suggestions; Josh Steiner who became my computer guru; Timothy Bigham for his excellent proof work; Rick Schmitz for the photo that makes me look like I can still play; Bill Porter and Mike Haines for the wealth of old photos of long ago heroes.

Thanks to the people who trusted me to take the reins of their events; Richie Florence, Chuck and Mike Markulis, Matt Braun, Jeff Bey, Greg Sullivan, Mark Griffin, Shannon Daulton, George Hardie, Robert Turner, Mark Betor, Taro Ito, Leo Chu, Mick McMillan, Barbara Woodward, Gil and Andee Atkisson, Torben Gramstrup, Pat Murray and Jim Bakula.

And then there are those who inspired me by sheer example; Mike Shamos, Bob Jewett, Bob Byrne, Jerry Breisath, Barry Behrman, Barry Hearns, Frank Bartolini, Barry Dubow and Paul Balukas.

Two friends who have made a huge difference in my life are Christopher Easley and Eric "Fatboy" Petersen. Chris came to work for me at age eighteen in my first pool room and became a life long friend. He has consistently been there to support me in all my endeavors. Fatboy is responsible for making me get off my ass and write this book. He said that I had some great stories to tell and they would make a good book. He pestered me until I started writing. Thanks!

There are far too many players to thank. I have attempted to do that by remembering them in this book. Without them I would have no story to tell.

And last a very big thank you to Mike Howerton and Jerry Forsyth for creating AZ Billiards, my second home the last four years. It was on their billiard website that I found my voice and realized that there were many fans who truly enjoyed hearing about a golden era in pool and the players of that generation. It was the AZ crowd who finally convinced me to create a written legacy about my years in pool. Thank you all so much!

None of the names contained herein have been changed to protect the innocent. I felt that the only way to properly tell the following stories was to use everyone's real name, and let the chips fall where they may. Some of my stories are flattering and some are not. I share these stories from the point of view of a participant and as a witness to what took place. There is nothing I say here that I wouldn't say to anyone's face.

IN THE BEGINNING

The modern era of Pool began with the release of the movie *The Hustler* in 1961. This classic film by Robert Rossen starred Paul Newman, Jackie Gleason, George C. Scott and Piper Laurie in the lead roles. It triggered a reaction among young men all across the country, who decided to pick up a cue and emulate Paul Newman's character, "Fast Eddie", and become pool players.

This influx of new players and fresh blood brought life back to a game that had been in the doldrums throughout the 50's. Pool had enjoyed remarkable popularity in the 1920's, with dozens of large palatial poolrooms to be found in cities across America. The Depression closed many of them, with a small resurgence during the Second World War. Following the war years, there was a gradual slide in poolroom business, and tournaments became almost nonexistent.

Then came *The Hustler*, and new modern rooms began popping up everywhere. This was a Godsend to existing players, whose livelihood depended on finding opponents to gamble with and win money from. The 60's became a time of relative prosperity for them, and new tournaments began to appear affording them another opportunity to make money.

The first of these was the aptly named Hustler's Tournament, put on by the Jansco Brothers in the Southern Illinois hamlet of Johnston City. What began as an exclusively One Pocket event in 1961 quickly evolved into an All Around tournament in 1962 featuring One Pocket, 9-Ball and Straight Pool. It lasted three weeks and attracted every self respecting pool player and hustler in the country.

Emerging on a parallel path was a close friend of the Janscos, a man known in pool circles as "New York Fats". He now resided nearby in the even smaller village of Dowell, Illinois. He had met and married a local beauty queen, and they set up a homestead, from which he branched out across the Little Egypt area of Southern Illinois in gambling forays.

Fats, Jay and Mike (Fat's agent)

THE MINNESOTA FATS SAGA

The Hustler was a great novel written by Walter Tevis in 1959. It told the story of aspiring pool hustler Fast Eddie Felson and his monumental match with "Minnesota Fats". The characters were based on fictitious pool players, created by the fertile imagination of Tevis. He had traveled around Ohio and Kentucky visiting the "action" pool rooms, and getting a taste of the hustler's life style. Then he made up his story.

Not so, said Rudolf Wanderone Jr. from New York City. I am the real Minnesota Fats, and he proudly proclaimed this news at a drive-in movie theater outside Johnston City, Illinois, which was featuring *The Hustler.* The year was 1961 and the theater was owned by Fat's buddy, George Jansco. Local media types thought this might make an interesting story, so they gave this boastful "fat man" some press. One thing led to another and pretty soon the national media picked up the story. It didn't hurt that the movie was a huge box office success.

Fats was helped by his sheer girth, and the fact that Willie Mosconi got on the band wagon and denied Wanderone's claims. Mosconi said that this fat man was actually New York Fats, not Minnesota Fats. If anything, these denials helped Wanderone establish some credibility as a hustler of some renown. The crafty Fats picked up on this and pressed his claims. He threatened to sue Tevis and 20th Century Fox who released the film. This led to counter claims by Tevis, and abject denials that he had ever met this New York Fats character. All these claims and counter claims were duly covered by the national media.

It finally had to be settled in court. The court battle made front page news across the nation for several weeks in 1962. In the end Tevis' version was concurred with by the court, but like it or not, New York Fats was reborn as Minnesota Fats. Wanderone continued to use that name the rest of his life, and capitalized on his celebrity in every way possible. Tevis went to his death bed claiming there was no such character in real life, but it made little difference to Fats' adoring public.

JOHNSTON CITY AND THE STARDUST

These were a series of memorable tournaments put on by George and Paulie Jansco from 1961 to 1972. The first Johnston City tournament in 1961 was strictly a One Pocket affair, with a small field of select players. It was won by Johnny Vevis, and the self proclaimed Minnesota Fats finished second. In the ensuing years it was played as an "All Around" event with One Pocket, Nine Ball and Straight Pool divisions. Due to the success of these tourneys, the Janscos were encouraged to start a similar event, held at the Stardust Casino in Las Vegas. This tournament ran from 1965 through 1973.

George Jansco was a man of great *influence* in his neck of the woods. Following his demise in 1971, his less well connected brother Paulie tried to continue the tradition, but was met with one setback after another. The final straw was when Federal agents raided the 1972 tournament, and arrested all the players for gambling. The Stardust tourney continued for one more year, before it too was cancelled forever. Both these tournaments, and their coverage by ABC's Wide World Of Sports, had fueled a resurgence in tournament pool.

By the 1970's professional pool players had several major tournaments they could compete in each year. Surrounding each of these events was some healthy "back room" action, where the real money changed hands. Before I go any further, let me share with you a list I compiled long ago chronicling the winners of these memorable tournaments.

JOHNSTON CITY			
YEAR	ONE POCKET	NINE BALL	STRAIGHT POOL
1962	Marshall Carpenter	Luther Lassiter	Luther Lassiter
1963	Eddie Taylor	Luther Lassiter	Luther Lassiter
1964	Eddie Taylor	Luther Lassiter	Luther Lassiter
1965	Larry Johnson	Harold Worst	Harold Worst
1966	Eddie Kelly	Eddie Kelly	Joe Balsis
1967	Larry Johnson	Luther Lassiter	Irving Crane
1968	Larry Johnson	Danny Jones	Al Coslosky
1969	Luther Lassiter	Luther Lassiter	Joe Russo
1970	Ronnie Allen	Keith Thompson	Luther Lassiter
1971	Jim Rempe	Jimmy Marino	Luther Lassiter
1972	Larry Johnson	Billy Incardona	Danny Diliberto

STARDUST OPEN			
YEAR	ONE POCKET	NINE BALL	STRAIGHT POOL
1965	Harold Worst	Eddie Kelly	Irving Crane
1966	Larry Johnson	Ronnie Allen	Cisero Murphy
1967	Eddie Taylor	Danny Jones	Mike Eufemia
1968	Marvin Henderson	Irving Crane	Joe Balsis
1969	Danny Gartner	Joe Balsis	Steve Mizerak
1970	Steve Cook	Bernie Schwartz	Joe Russo
1971	Johnny Ervolino	Luther Lassiter	Joe Balsis
1972	Bill Staton	Jimmy Mataya	Pete Margo
1973	Johnny Ervolino	Norman Hitchcock	Larry Johnson (Eight Ball)

A BLAST FROM THE PAST

There were many memorable moments that took place during my various expeditions to the "Wonderland" of Pool, circa 1960's. Some of them I reminisced about in my short lived column for the National Billiard News, entitled *Diary Of A Pool Hustler*. I will give these columns an 'encore' appearance here, and throw in one about the Dayton tournament for good measure.

This first one appeared in the National Billiard News in 1974. Please remember, I wrote these over thirty years ago. Errors and typos remain intact.

"Never Never Land"

When I was a young man courting the pool table way back in 1963, I talked a few of my friends into taking a trip to Johnston City. Johnston City, Illinois was that magnet of a small town that hosted the annual Hustler's Pool Tournament. I had heard of what was happening there and I didn't want to miss a thing. When we got on the road I wouldn't let them stop to eat. I was in a hurry, no doubt about it a pool freak heading for Mecca.

In ten hours we were there. But where .... the middle of nowhere, Illinois. It took a genuine pool room detective just to find the place. A small building just outside the town limits under a neon sign spelling out Jansco's Show Bar. We pulled into a sardine type parking lot, packed with cars from all over...at least thirty different states....and the shudder of expectation of what was happening took over my entire being. At this point my memories are rather blurry, but there are indelibles imprinted on my mind and I can still see the crowds of people, hear the noise and feel the excitement.

We all crammed into the tournament room and tried to get a glimpse of the four top players doing battle on the two tables set side by side. I don't remember who played but it was the time of the Knoxville Bear, Squirrel, and Luther Lassiter was top dog. I loved every minute of it.

When the matches ended the spectators and players moved in the direction of the 'practice room'. This was an adjacent building that must have been a converted garage. Not at all impressive on the outside but on the inside pure gold nine ball, a player's paradise. With wall to wall people eyeballing the wizardry of players who were legends in their own time.

On the first table to the right of the door, Ronnie Allen was playing Mr. Cokes "one hand up in the air" One Pocket for a thousand a rattle. Next to them was the match that took five years to finish. Bill Staton, the Weenie Beenie man, and Harold Worst the best man to ever pick up a cue in my book, were trying to beat a seemingly impossible proposition game, getting ten to one odds on a hundred dollar bet. And in the back room of the same building Cuban Joe was playing Jack Perkins a three thousand dollar session of One Pocket. If that's not delicious enough, for dessert we had a ring nine ball game ($50 a man) featuring some fair country shooters like Jimmy Moore, The Bear, Boston Shorty, Detroit Whitey and New York Blackie.

Almost too much for a 19 year old pool nut to stand, but still savoring every ball click. I joined a crowd of about twenty guys cozying back and forth from room to room trying to keep tabs on all the games at one time. Looking back in retrospect, I feel we were all part of something real, no pretense on the part of any of the players, a genuine shoot out, no holds barred. It was a tough game for me at the time, I had difficulty making more than four balls in a row.

Ronnie and Cokes were the big attraction. A brash, cocky kid from California by way of Oklahoma against an old war horse from everywhere and anywhere. Ronnie was flashy and daring, playing loose and wide open, seemingly oblivious to the pressure of the high stakes. With all eyes focused on him, Ronnie seemed to gather momentum and he obviously welcomed the mass adulation of the crowd. Cokes was placid and quiet, much like a shrewd General surveying a battle plan. Old Hubert was in complete control of himself and his game. Regardless of his obvious age he had an overwhelming presence about him. The combination of his stature, dignity and low key power of intelligence made him the dominating figure in the room.

Through the sheer genius of his vast experience he held the onrushing Allen off game after game before he finally quit from exhaustion. Cokes was on the short end three games and Ronnie had made a score but it was a split decision on who was the better of the two.

In another part of the action room, Harold Worst was giving the proposition game entrepreneur fits, making one amazing shot after another. With Beenie coaching him on problem shots how could he go wrong? Just listening to their patter on which shot to shoot, how to hit it and where to

Bill "Weenie Beenie" Staton

"Cornbread Red" Billy Burge

go afterwards was an education in itself. Beenie might say, "Make the six ball with a little low left english, dive under the fourteen and slide around the eleven ball, catch the end rail, tickle the nine and stop for the ten next." Wonder of wonders, Harold would do just that and say, "Is that okay Beenie?" Needless to say they busted the guy and he hasn't been back since. His proposition game beat all the other players but Harold and Beenie sent him home for good.

Meanwhile the Cuban was going off for a telephone number in the back room. Solid Jack Perkins did him in. He ran eight and out so many times I lost count. Of course in later years the Cuban was to become one of the game's most consistent winners.

In the nine ball ring game Cowboy Jimmy Moore was smooth stroking rack after rack. Fresh players kept coming into the game to replace the departed financially embarrassed losers. No one could slow the Cowboy down that night, for he was playing super pool from beginning to end and took them all down good. He shot so well the other players barred him from anymore nine ball action that year. That's the greatest trophy a money player can brag about....When they don't let you play there is nothing more to say.

The End

This second piece is from the same era, the mid 70's, and it's about the most memorable hustler of them all.

"CORNBREAD RED"

That's right, Cornnnn Breaddddd Reddddd.......Pool hustling entrepreneur. A magician with the lip and the stick. Red will play and he will bet high. He'll bring money out of all four pockets anytime he can get the action. Red is in his own league, a gambling superstar! Tales about him permeate the pool world. The pool players grapevine has carried accounts of his exploits to the farthest reaches of this country. Who is this character behind all these stories?

He's a wiry fortyish man with a close cropped headful of red hair. His body is slightly bent in a pool player's crouch even when he's standing. Sort of like he's ready to play anytime. His personality is a blend of Okie and Midwesterner, but his style is distinctly his own. Red really lays down the conversation. When you rap to him it's no holds barred. Any facet of your life may be brought out in public for examination, if Red's mind gives his tongue the message. He holds nothing back. Red tells it like it is, in spades.

Using a combination of the variances of the English language, he expresses himself verbally as well as anyone I've ever seen. Anybody can understand the meaning and intent of his words, although the way he delivers them is pure Cornbread Red. His moods are as changeable as a gambler's fortunes. He can gravitate from being your best friend to your worst enemy and back again in the course of a sentence. That's how strong Red puts it down...Top Speed!

And his wide open style carries over naturally to his pool game. Red gets completely loose on a pool table. Pool is a piece of cake to him. It's his shortcut through life. He's found the secret. It's true in life just as in pool. Stay loose and relaxed and everything seems easy. Get tight and things get tough. Red is at ease with himself, he's the master of his own destiny.

The Cornbread Red approach to life is best exemplified by the following two excerpts. The first recalls a time in Las Vegas when Red's balls-out gambling style busted the crap tables at the Stardust. The score was unreal, too much to count. So what did Red do with his newly found fortune? He went directly to the men's clothing store in the hotel and proceeded to buy all his friends (that included everyone present) anything they wanted. The store ran out of clothes before Red ran out of money. That is the classic Redbird philosophy for investing his money. And who is to say, it may pay the greatest dividends in the long run.

The second incident took place in Detroit, Red's home base. A hot shot young nine ball player from out West (guess?) came to town with a flush backer. The sky was the limit. The word went out that the kid wanted to play Red $1,000 nine ball. Red's horse called him at home and woke Red. He explained the situation to Red and wanted to know how to handle it. Red asked him how much they had. The reply was $10,000. Red said okay, tell the kid he would come down to the room right now on one condition. They play $10,000 a game! Needless to say when the kid heard this he couldn't find the door fast enough. Just the thought of a $10,000 game of nine ball turned him to silly putty.

You better believe it. Ole Corn's as clever as a politician and reckless as Evel Knievel with a one ton heart to make it all work. He's got an act you don't want to miss.

The End

Okay I got one more for you.

Nobody who was there will soon forget it. Everywhere you looked there were luminaries of the hustler's world. Wimpy and Canton Don cutting up with Detroit Whitey over there; Jersey Red and Shorty reminiscing over here; Frisco Jack and Richie at the card table; Bugs and Youngblood burning up some banks; Two Hippy Jimmy's knocking heads at Nine Ball; and in the feature of this **Ten Ring Circus** was Ronnie, trying to fade the graduates of *Cochran's School of Pay Ball.* And the prize pupil, Magna Cum Laude Denny took it all down in the end.

It was the last few gypsies trying to get a respite from the straight 9 to 5 world that was overwhelming the land. But it was the same world that gave birth to these gypsies and that fed and clothed them. As long as the basic structure of society promoted personal greed, then the Professional Gambler (Gypsy) was guaranteed a haven. He would always have a spot to go to and a mark to beat. A mark was anyone, anywhere, who because of his own fears decided to take a chance and lost.

Dayton in 1974 was a condensed version of what was happening all over the country. It was an opportunity to gather together and sharpen our teeth. It was a cram course for the rookies and a refresher for the veterans. Everybody learned, some just paid a higher price for the knowledge.

In the tournament, which was secondary to the gathering, Buddy Hall started like a flash in all three divisions and hung on to capture the nine ball title. Ray Martin, playing smoothly and confidently came out of the loser's bracket for second place. Youngblood played better as the crowds got bigger and ego'd his way to the bank pool trophy. Jimmy Fusco showed his powerful stroke had made him a threat in any game as he took the runnerup spot. But the unofficial Bank Pool Champion of the era remained Mr. Bugs. Tall and handsome, the quiet man made even the most hardened players stare in amazement as he ran those seven and eights.

In the One Pocket, Jimmy Marino snuck in for the gold with Larry Lisciotti displaying his expertise to finish second. The playoff for the all around title was All Hall. Buddy played superbly and deserved to be recognized as the Champion in '74. It was a great tournament, a great time and an experience I'm glad I didn't miss.

The End

A youthful Billy Incardona

"Bucktooth"

HIGH ROLLING IN VEGAS

I saw many big money games in Vegas at the Stardust but two of them stand out. The first was between "St. Louis Suts", a heavy set building contractor, who loved to play Pool and bet high. His adversaries included Larry Perkins, his cousin Jack, Puggy Pearson and Nicky Vacchiano, a noted Vegas gambler out of Philadelphia. The game was One Pocket and the bet was humongous. The year was 1968 and they were playing single games for anywhere from six to eight thousand dollars, a decent annual salary back then.

Suts had huge wads of money in every pocket, and the bet was determined by which wad he pulled out. He would literally throw the money on the table, and say match it. If it was eight thousand, then the assembled gamblers would all take a piece of the action, until they had the full amount covered, and then Suts and Larry Perkins would play one game for the whole pile.

The Vegas "crew" was winning game after game, with Suts occasionally pulling an upset. At one point Suts refused to play Perkins anymore, and insisted that someone else take over. Puggy Pearson took up the sword and continued the pummeling. They played over the course of two days, and when the smoke cleared, the Vegas gang had made a score in excess of one hundred thousand dollars. In 1960's dollars this was monstrous, a real fortune; like winning a million dollars today.

The second game I witnessed, was also my introduction to the loud mouth braggart known as "Bucktooth". The reason for the nickname was obvious, as his front teeth protruded in a massive over-bite. Still I found this name quite offensive, and couldn't understand why it didn't upset him to be referred to in this manner. The name some clown had labeled me with, "Toupee Jay", still rankled me whenever I heard it. It took me many years to come to terms with this pool nickname I had inadvertently earned.

Bucktooth had managed to get a straight shooting youngster out of Pittsburgh to give him the *six ball* spot in a game of 9-Ball. This meant the 'Tooth could win on the six or the nine, and Pittsburgh Billy could win only on the nine. It was a massive spot for a player of 'Tooth's obvious skill. The game began for $100 a rack, a very big game at that time. There was ample side betting both ways, so it was not hard to make a 'sweat bet' and I did. I bet $20 a game on 'Tooth and was winning for a while. After a few hours of this, Billy caught a higher gear and began to run out almost every time he had a shot. They were playing *push out* 9-Ball back then, and 'Tooth would often push out for a very long bank shot, and Billy would rifle it in and run out. 'Tooth continued to push out for long rail banks, and Billy continued pounding them in. 'Tooth could not believe what he was seeing, and kept asking to raise the bet. I couldn't believe it either, but when I had lost back all my winnings, I decided to switch sides and bet on Billy.

By now it was early in the morning, and the bet had reached $300 a game. Billy was playing in jeans and a flimsy tank top that showed off his healthy torso. He had a well developed athlete's body. At some point the hard working Billy Incardona removed his tank top and played bare-chested for the last few hours. He wasn't missing a ball now. Banks, combinations, long cut shots, billiards, everything was splitting the wicket, and he was winning game after game.

But Bucktooth would not quit. He left twice to go down to the cage and reload. Finally at about 9 AM Bucktooth went dry for the last time. He paid off Billy for the last game and told him he was broke. Billy had won over $20,000 playing $300 9-Ball. He never looked back after that, piling score upon score for the next thirty years. Bucktooth returned to his home in Oakland and went into the jewelry and furniture businesses. He made millions over the course of the next few years, and eventually returned to the world of high stakes pool. But he never barked at Billy Incardona again.

Billy Incardona today

WINKS POOL HALL

I started out at Winks Pool Hall during the early 60's. I had seen *The Hustler,* and like so many others I was captivated by Eddie Felson, the fierce loner and anti-hero, portrayed so capably by Paul Newman. Now I wanted to play pool, somewhere, anywhere. Sadly that was almost nowhere in Dayton, Ohio in the early 60's. You had to be eighteen to get in the poolrooms, so I was on the outside looking in.

I did get to play occasionally at my friend's house, whose father was a champion golfer and former pool player, or so it was rumored. We would sneak into the attic, where the full size pool table was tucked away, and bang balls around until his Dad came home and shooed us away. It wasn't much of a pool fix, but it would have to do, until I could figure out another path to degradation. I had tried sneaking into the illustrious Red, White and Blue poolroom in downtown Dayton, and had actually witnessed a money game in session once. But the proprietor made it imminently clear to me that the next time he saw me in there, I would be severely reprimanded, as in beaten to a pulp!

My only other choice was Winks, a den of iniquity that was hidden away in the back of a shopping center called Forest Park Plaza. One small problem; the same laws were in effect there, and I was a youthful looking sixteen year old. I couldn't fool anyone into thinking I was eighteen, but "Pappy" Winkler (that's what they called him) was a larcenous old gent, and he figured if the kids had money, let 'em slip in for a game or two, or three or four. So he would let us youngsters play in the back of the room after school, but he kicked us out in time to get home for dinner. He didn't want any problems with parents demanding his closure.

That's where I saw my first hustlers up close; Frank Reeves, Whitey Stone, Bill Phelps, Dino the Jeweler, Tex Shively, Fat Pat, Homer the Cook, New York Maurie, Pete Glenn, Patcheye, Valley Street Red and many more characters who left an indelible impression on me, and my wallet.

I loved hanging around with these guys, and listening to their stories of thievery and mayhem. I just wanted to be one of the 'boys'. You know, another accepted thief and gambler. What ambition I had!

Early on I knew I was no match for any of these real pool players. I mean I could hardly make a ball, let alone run out. So I contented myself with watching them play, and gamble among themselves, and anyone else who dared to mix with them. One who dared was a big mouthed gambler from Mansfield, Ohio named Bill Stigall. He was quite a player too. Stigall had come in once or twice before, and won money at Winks. Little did Bill know what was in store for him on his next venture to Dayton's Promised Land.

Stigall returned early one Friday evening, and loudly announced he was ready to play anyone for any amount. A call was made to "Valley Street Red", and soon enough he came sauntering in, 250 pounds of adult baby fat, tucked into an ill fitting tee shirt, with oversized jeans dangling on his abundant hips. A cherubic grin was etched on his face, and a disorderly tuft of red hair topped off this strange permutation of humanity. But he could play! And that's what counts.

A discussion ensued between Red and Stigall. What was the game? What was the bet? Who would hold the money? ....etc., etc. Finally all was agreed upon, and some hapless looking dolt was made to sit by the table, and hold the lordly sum of $600 ($300 apiece) in his shirt pocket. The game began and Stigall quickly pulled into the lead. After about five or six games, a large man burst into the poolroom, waving a gun in the air. Everyone, myself included, ducked under the pool tables. The angry man was shouting the name of the poor fellow who was holding the stakes. I felt genuinely sorry for this guy, who was frozen in his chair. I knew I was about to witness a killing.

When the gunman spotted the guy he was looking for, he ran over to him, demanding the money he was owed. He was shouting and waving the gun in his face. The guy was obviously scared shitless. He kept saying he didn't have it, but would pay him when he did. At that moment the bad guy spotted the stack of bills protruding from his shirt pocket. He literally ripped the pocket off his shirt grabbing the money. The poor guy protested meekly, but what can you do when someone has a very large gun stuck in your face.

Now Bill Stigall jumped up from hiding, and protested that he was taking the stake money, for the game that was in progress. The gunman would have none of it, and pointed his gun at Stigall, shouting, "Get back! Get back!" And Bill got back! With that the man backed out of the poolroom, gun in one hand, money in the other, and disappeared into the night. No one was inclined to pursue him down the hallway leading away from Winks, not even Stigall, who just sat glumly in his chair staring at the man with the ripped shirt. After some sad meanderings about the hazards of 'road gambling', Bill packed up his cue and headed home to Mansfield.

That experience had been the most frightening of my young life, or at least it was for one day. The next night I wandered into Winks, and who do I see sitting together at the card table. It was none other than the gunman, the stakeholder, Valley Street Red and a couple of other outlaws who I recognized. They were all laughing and joking, all buddy-buddy like. What the heck was going on here? This scene was boggling my mind. I had to ask my friend Frank to explain it all to my innocent ears. He pulled me aside and whispered the essence of the plot to me. It was all one big charade to screw Stigall out of his cash. For the first time I realized there were real outlaws hanging around at Winks. It wasn't all tough talk and make believe.

Joe Kerr, a very young Earl Strickland, Joe Burns, Buddy Hall

Joe Burns bought Winks from Pappy Winkler and renamed it
Forest Park Billiards.

OKLAHOMA UNIVERSITY

My lifelong pool odyssey had begun. The next ten years of my life would amount to a total obsession with pool, my only desire being to play night and day. At that point nothing else mattered, just wake up and go to the pool hall. I was eighteen and a pool room bum in the making.

Unfortunately, college got in the way. My upstanding and well established parents insisted I get a college education. Even though I was sick of school, I had no choice. My only option was being able to choose the college I wanted to attend. Most of my friends were going somewhere nearby; The University of Dayton, Ohio State, Cincinnati, Ohio U., Bowling Green, Miami of Ohio, etc., etc. I wanted out of here. I was sick of Dayton with its cold winters and all the hard working suckers. I knew I was smarter than any of them, and I was going to prove it.

I chose Oklahoma University mainly because it was far away from the life I had always known. I was looking for fun and adventure, and new worlds to conquer. So here I was in Norman, Oklahoma; a stranger in a strange land, a city boy surrounded by country folks. I liked them! Everyone was open and friendly, and they had this down home humor that was refreshing to me. I liked everything about Oklahoma except attending classes. So I did my best to avoid them as much as possible.

All I wanted and craved was a little money and a pool game. My Freshman year was a mix of sporadic classroom attendance, sprinkled with visits to the three pool rooms I could find in Norman, plus the Union Building with its array of pool tables, and one illustrious student named Tommy Fisher. Why Tommy was at O.U. I couldn't quite determine at the time. Only years later did it dawn on me that he was there primarily for the soft pickings at pool and cards, me included. Tommy taught me One Pocket (expensive) and he also showed me a thing or two about Gin Rummy (more expensive).

I decided early on that it was far better for me to join up with Tommy than to do battle with him. One weekend we decided to journey into Oklahoma City and see what action we could hustle up. Mistake number two! Holding court in OKC at the time was none other than one Norman Hitchcock. He might as well have been Wyatt Earp, since he shot Tommy so full of holes. I was relegated to playing Bevo, an octogenarian who was nearly deaf and blind as well. A perfect match for me, and I was kind enough to make a few small donations to his trust fund.

All this was taking place at the Central Club, in the heart of the Downtown district. It was much like Winks; a place for ne'er-do-wells, hustlers, outlaws and the permanently unemployed to gather. I felt right at home. I came back time and time again to partake in small stakes pool action, cards and even dominoes. I'm quite certain I never won once, but what a wonderful education I was getting in the mean time.

At dear old O.U., needing additional funding, my roommate Jim Herberick and me set up a business we entitled The Foodman. We would deliver food to the dormitories late at night, to sate the appetites of all the hungry students. We started out bringing sandwiches and drinks, in a basket we carried around our necks. There were no 7 Eleven's or all night stores in those days. We were the only choice for the ravenous students. Our business quickly grew, and within a few months we had a dozen employees.

We gutted our two bedroom apartment and remade it into a food preparation area. The living room had two long tables set side by side, with two girls busy making sandwiches all day long. All our supplies were stored in one bedroom (along with an extra frig.) and Jim and I shared the other. Jim was the cook, with roast beef and turkey our staples. We also had bologna and cheese sandwiches for the less affluent. A hungry student could get a roast beef sandwich for 65 cents, turkey was 55 cents, and you could get bologna and cheese for 45 cents. Such a deal! And we offered fresh milk (chocolate or regular)

or orange juice for a quarter. That was the entire menu, until we added small fried pies (30 cents) for dessert. By now we had ten guys on routes; a few guys in the dorms, two for all the 'frat' houses, two more for sorority houses, a couple to hit the married student housing and even one for faculty housing. We were in 'tall cotton' now, each of us pulling in over $500 a week. Big money in the 60's! A few months of this, and I was really getting pumped up. I had a new Corvette and a real bank account, not just money stashed under my t-shirts.

Then bureaucracy reared its ugly head. I was called into a meeting with the Dean of Men, since I was technically still enrolled as a student. When he inquired whether we were making a profit, I boasted that my partner and I were pulling a thousand a week out of this operation. His eyes spun around like pinballs. I should have realized that this career educator was making far less. He came down hard after that. The Dean informed me, in no uncertain terms, that my business must be licensed and approved to operate in the city of Norman. Otherwise, c'est la vie.

I went to the city license bureau in Norman and they were surprisingly nice. They said an inspector would come out and check our operation to see if it met with their standards. If all went well, they would issue us a license. Cool! At the duly appointed time, the Inspector came to the home base of The Foodman; our apartment in the large complex. My partner and I greeted him warmly, and proudly showed how we had converted the apartment into a food making operation. He was quite impressed and also very nice. There was only one small problem. We were informed that you cannot do this in residential housing. Bummer!

He suggested that we make an arrangement with an existing restaurant in town, to use their facilities to prepare our sandwiches. Great, we were sunk. But God bless Jim Herberick (who also bought a new Corvette) wherever you are. He went into town and found a restaurant that opened for dinner at 5 PM. We made a deal to come in from 9 AM until 4 PM and make our sandwiches. We got our license!

All was well, except the success of The Foodman was really cutting into my pool time. I had a new car and a few thousand in the bank. I wanted to play pool, not work. So I found a solution. The first employee we had hired, a guy named Gene, had asked me once or twice before to buy in as a partner. I had refused him every time. Now we sat down to talk in earnest. I wanted out, did he want to buy The Foodman? I told him I wanted $15,000 and he could have it. Deal!

Gene somehow came up with $7,500 down and I was off the hook. Jim stayed on as his partner, and the other $7,500 was owed to him. I wasn't such a dummy after all. Now I had beaucoup bucks, a good car and a nice cue. World, here I come! Bye bye O.U. and thanks! I had enjoyed my two years there, and the little I had learned in the classrooms. My real education was in the business world. I found out that there was money to be made if you were enterprising enough.

HUSTLING OKLAHOMA

I loaded some clothes, my cue, a Browning .25 and a pile of cash, and I was off and running; a pool scuff looking for action. Back to Oklahoma City first and the friendly confines of the Central Club, with all the usual hustler types I had grown accustomed to. I became a regular there, and began to hear about the soft action around town. It had to be better than the Central Club because I was still the low man on this totem pole. So I took off with

20

my fellow college dropout and pool bum Mike Vaught, and we hit the rooms around OKC. In these family oriented poolrooms, that were all the rage in the 60's, we found easy pickings; mostly young kids trying to learn how to play, and we were *veterans* with a few years under our belt. It was all nickel and dime action though, and I was getting restless quick.

I was also scavenging the many bars that had small tables, made to order for a short stroker like me. Then one day I ran into "Herman the German" and "Little Hand", going at it for $25 a game. I knew that I wasn't in their class yet, so I forged a new game plan. It was time to *discover* Oklahoma. My first stop was Chickasha and I hit the bar scene there. I played a couple of guys and made a few bucks, and they recommended I go to Lawton for bigger games. Lawton was a town loaded with bars and Indians. And they liked to drink and gamble. I was in heaven.

I played from bar to bar for a few days and was beating everybody, when I finally met Dwayne, a young Indian sharpshooter. All the big chiefs were betting on this straight shooting kid, who must have been all of eighteen. We played Eight Ball for ten and twenty a game until the bar closed. I was winning about a hundred and they asked me to come to the reservation where they had a bar table. Sure, why not. A very stupid move as it turned out. Have you ever been on an Indian reservation late on a Saturday night? The bar is open, everyone is drunk and it's chaotic to say the least.

But they did have a table, and soon Dwayne and I were hard at it, with a zillion Indians crowded around sweating the action. They were loud, they were ornery and they were drunk. And I was the only white man in the joint! Smart move huh! I realized pretty quickly that winning was not an option here. Getting out alive was now my goal. I quietly dumped a few games to Dwayne and told him I was getting tired. He gave me a knowing smile and bless his little red heart, he said we could quit after the next game, which I promptly lost. A few of the Indians didn't want me to go, since I was losing every game. But I thanked them profusely and told them I would come back soon. Dwayne and his friend escorted me to my car and helped me escape. Whew, lesson learned.

A LITTLE CINCY, A LITTLE NEW YORK

I was pretty much done with all that Oklahoma had to offer, so I returned to the friendly confines of home and Dayton. I had moved up the pecking order and was now considered one of the "shortstops" around town. I hung in the rooms and played all night, usually returning home about the time my dad was heading off to work. This got old quick and soon I was shunted off to Ohio State for another go at college. I had a go all right, in every pool room in Columbus. My favorite was one run by "Handsome" Danny Jones and it was full of hustlers. My kind of place!

This lasted one semester and when my parents found out I was not attending classes, they sent me to Cincinnati to work at the Fifth-Third Bank Building in the rental office. My dad was a minor partner in the ownership of the building. Naturally I found the best poolroom in town, Mergards. I became a regular there and continued my education in pool. I got to hang out with Joey Spaeth and Cincinnati Clem every night, and listen to their stories of the road. I was playing too, every night till closing. I'd go home, sleep a few hours, get up and go to work, and do it all again.

Then the Fifth-Third Bank building was sold, and I got my next job in New York working in my Uncle's real estate office. I reported to work every day at nine and hit the poolrooms every day at five, like clockwork. I thought I could play by now. How sadly mistaken I was. I'd heard about the fabled 7/11 pool room and couldn't get in there fast enough. I got passed around between Jersey Red, New York Blackie, Boston Shorty, Richie from the Bronx, Brooklyn Johnny and the ultimate New York hustler, Rex. They took turns emptying me out. I never asked for a spot, and played all these champions dead even. I had a lot to learn!

This routine got old fast, and I decided to see what else was out there. There was a lot! McGirr's, Broadway Billiards, and my all time favorite nesting place, Guys and Dolls on 50th St. This became my pool home in New York. I loved Guys and Dolls; it was big and juicy, with action everywhere. If you came in here to play, you were expected to gamble. And gamble I did, but I was becoming a little more discreet in my game making. I avoided the players and found some lesser lights to prey upon. There were out of work actors, various salesmen and Manhattan rich kids that hung in there also. I fit right in with this crowd, except I could play a little now. The last three years of bouncing around had seasoned me.

I learned two important things in New York that helped me ferret out the right games. Don't play Straight Pool with old men and don't play Banks with black guys. Avoiding these two pitfalls were the key to me making the right games with the right people. I lasted less than a year there before tragedy befell me.

"Jersey Red" Jack Breit

"Richie from the Bronx" Ambrose

THE ARMY BECKONS

This was the 60's and if a young man wasn't married or in school he was a candidate for the military. I got the call and was summarily sent to Fort Polk, Louisiana. The Hell Hole of the South would be a compliment for that place. In the summer of '66 it was a furnace down there, with our days spent getting in shape and learning how to kill our fellow man. Our Drill Sergeant was a big Indian (yes, another one) who hated everyone and was set on one thing; making our lives miserable. And he was good at it!

Lucky for me I scored the highest in the company on our written tests, and after Basic Training I was sent to Supply Clerks school. Nearly everyone else in the company went to "Tigerland" for Advanced Infantry Training. That was followed by a thirteen month stint in Viet Nam. I ducked 'Nam and saved my skin. Another close call avoided. I would become the Supply Clerk for the 387th Transportation Unit. On the weekends we got leave and I went into nearby Leesville for some R&R. My idea of R&R was to find a pool game, and the town was full of bars and soldiers playing pool for money. This town was infinitely better than anyplace I'd been before, and on payday weekend I made out like a bandit.

Eventually I branched out to Alexandria and Lake Charles looking for games. Someone actually tried to match me up with a young Steve Mizerak, who was in school nearby. He strolled into the room one day and I scatted out the back door. I had already caught his act and wanted no part of him.

I got out of there in late 1967, just in time to make it up to Johnston City. This time I made a few games and got more involved in things. I played Benny 'The Goose' Conway on a bar table in the Show Bar and he stuck it to me. I saw what a good bar player looked like, and I wasn't there yet.

Then I got hustled by Omaha Fats, who remembered me from previous years. He played me Six Ball for $2 a game, and after I won three or four games, he quit on me. It was so funny to hear him call me "Mister", and ask for a spot. Fats was there, and so was everyone else, including the gang of killers from 7/11. They all greeted me fondly now; I was finally 'one of the boys'.

THE ROAD HEADS SOUTH

After a short visit back home, I decided to head south to visit my brother Bruce, who was enrolled in Medical School at Florida University. After all, he had visited me at Fort Polk. It was the least I could do. I took the long way in my 'Vette, stopping in Memphis and St. Louis, because I heard there was good action there. I was becoming a winning player, and only remember losing to Richie Austin in Memphis. I headed south through Mobile, Baton Rouge and New Orleans, playing all the way. I was winning more than losing, and all the time getting better. The heat of competition does that to you. By the time I got to Gainesville I had gone up another speed or two.

Bruce was the exact opposite of me, an academic who was going somewhere in life besides the poolroom. But he loved me dearly, and always looked out for his baby brother. We had done some Go-Kart racing as kids, then gravitated into motorcycles and drag racing. Bruce built an X-Dragster (with a four cylinder motor) as his Senior year project, and the car won its class at the first Indy Nationals in 1962. He was still into cars, and owned a souped up 1963 Corvette and a BSA motorcycle. At least we had something in common. He would go to class and I would zoom around town on his bike. I may have visited him at the Med School hospital once or twice. Anything to do with school was boring to me. I wanted to play pool!

In Gainesville there was one old poolroom downtown, and I quickly got a rep there. I beat a couple of the locals and they sic'ed their best player on me. He could play, and we battled all day at $5 9-Ball. We ended up breaking even, but my fate was sealed there. My only other choice was the Florida U. student recreation center, and 9-Ball was not allowed there. But you could play Eight Ball or Straight Pool, two of my least favorite games. Hanging out there was a nice looking young lad, who would finish second to Nick Varner in the National Collegiate Championships a year or so later. John something, I believe. Sorry, I forgot his name, but not his game.

John played Straights, and pretty good too. The kids there were trying to promote a game between us, since I had already soaked them all at Eight Ball. I adamantly refused to play 14.1 and he wouldn't play me Eight Ball, so we had a stalemate. One enterprising youngster came up with the winning formula. We would play one set of each! A 'race to eight' in Eight Ball and 100 points of Straight Pool. $50 a set. I went for it, pretty confident I could beat him in Eight Ball. And I did, so I was on a 'free roll'.

25

Unfortunately the 14.1 was also going as expected, and I was on the short end of a 92-28 bashing when, lo and behold, my brother walked in.

Bruce had never seen me play, only heard me talk about it. I had been telling him how good a pool player I now was. Yikes! How embarrassing. He was going to see me getting pasted. John boy had already written me off this match, and he was toying with me now. It was my turn, and I was looking at an open shot. I made the ball and broke a few balls off the pack. Bruce smiled at me and gave a little wave. I proceeded to run the rest of the rack and set up a break shot. I was still waaaay behind. Something happened then that I will never forget. I blanked out everything else and totally focused on the balls. I was mad and didn't want my brother to see me lose.

I whacked the rack wide open, and quickly burned off the next rack. The boy who made the game was racking the balls for both of us. He gave me a funny look that made me think he was betting the other way. So be it! I felt powerful now and the pockets looked like buckets. I ran another rack, and then one more. I had lost count, I was just shooting. Finally the rack boy put the balls up again, and I heard him say the score was 92-90. I needed ten! BAM, the rack was open. John was fidgeting in his chair. I was giving my first victim the 'electric chair'. And it felt good being the executioner. I cleared the final nine balls and it was over. I had run 72 and out, my lifetime high run (to this day). But more important, I had made my brother proud of me.

For the rest of the day Bruce couldn't stop talking about how good I was, and how much he enjoyed watching me play. That was worth millions to me, far more than the hundred dollars I won that day. The next time Bruce and I got together was in the early 70's, when we went racing once more. He lost his life at Phoenix International Raceway on February 27, 1972, during a race. He was twenty nine and a medical doctor. I miss him every day.

MOVING WEST

From Florida I headed west. I was twenty two and felt like I could play anyone. I was now familiar with almost all the top players, and had no problem ducking them. I also figured that no matter how good a guy played, he had to show his speed to beat me. If a good player tried to stall against me, he was in trouble.

I worked my way back across the South, stopping to play in every large town or city along the way. My M.O. was to stop in a town and go to a phone booth. I would find the page with billiard rooms on it and rip it out (yeah, that was me). Then I would visit the one that looked the biggest, and walk right up to the counter and tell the houseman I was looking for a game. No beating around the bush for me. No long drawn out elaborate hustles. I wanted to play pool, and I didn't care who you got to play me.

More often than not they would ask me how I played, or was I a good player. My stock answer was that I played okay. And you know what. It worked! I rarely had to sit on my ass, waiting for someone to show up who wanted to play. Either they found me a game, or I was on my way down the road. I got games nearly everywhere, booking mostly winners. Sometimes easy, sometimes tough, but I was constantly in action and doing just fine. The tough games usually ended with me quitting even, after butting heads for several hours. The other games ended with me paying the time. And that's a good thing!

I would play nearly any game someone asked for. More often than not the game of choice was 9-Ball, but it was not unusual for someone to ask me to play Eight Ball. I liked this because it told me one of two things. He was either inexperienced, or he was primarily a bar table player. I did get guys who only wanted to play One Pocket or Banks, and that was fine as well. I even played games like Cribbage and Cut Throat, and ventured onto Snooker and Billiard tables a time or two. My attitude was that if I was a better player than my opponent, eventually I would get the hang of the game and the table, and win.

WELCOME TO CALIFORNIA

I arrived on the West Coast in the winter of '67. I'll never forget my first drive up the coast from San Diego to Los Angeles. It was a sunny and beautiful day with the temperature in the 70's. I immediately fell in love with California, and it remains the longest love affair of my life, forty years and still thriving.

I drove into the L.A. downtown area and found a weekly hotel room. From there I could branch out into the surrounding city, and find the best poolrooms and bars. At the time I had no idea how big this place was. It would take me the better part of five years to discover all the best spots in L.A. But trust me when I tell you, I was actively looking every day.

Thus began my total immersion into the world of pool. In Los Angeles I quickly gave up the premise of a normal life. Every day was about finding a game, and getting in action. I had no interest in the latest movies, good restaurants, meeting girls, politics, foreign affairs, the state of the nation or anything else. I just wanted to play pool every waking hour, and that's exactly what I did.

There was only one dingy poolroom in downtown Los Angeles called 4th and Main. I played in there a couple of times, and then I left it alone for the most part. The inhabitants of 4th and Main were the dregs of Los Angeles society, a motley crew of thieves and con men. Even for a seasoned hustler like me, it was a desolate and dangerous place.

I quickly discovered Ye Billiard Den in Hollywood and Celebrity Billiards nearby. Another place called Mothers was in the same vicinity. The 60's were heady days for pool, with a multitude of choices available. In the San Fernando Valley there was Chopstix, The House of Billiards, Big Mamas and North Hollywood Billiards. All good spots with plenty of players. Santa Monica had The Mecca and another House of Billiards. On the east side was The Golden Cue and Five Points, and to the south, The Billiard Palace and Charley Milliken's place. And this was only scratching the surface.

Tournament Billiards and Charley Neal's were in the ghetto, full of black champions. Many bowling alleys had tables, most notably Tropicana Lanes, Gage Bowl and Gardena Bowl. Long Beach had Beautiful Billiards, Blackjacks and The Hole. Every town had a poolroom back then. I was in pool Heaven. L.A. was a great spot to ply my trade in the roaring 60's. To top it off there must have been a few hundred good bar spots to excavate.

Soon after my arrival, I established my base in the Hollywood area, and Ye Billiard Den became my home room. It was full of aspiring actors and musicians, who had time on their hands between jobs and auditions. Other assorted entertainment types hung out there as well. Many sported personal cues, and liked to fancy themselves hustlers of sorts. Easy pickings for a hardened five year veteran of pool fracases from coast to coast.

I made my daily bread in The Den, as it was called. Fairly soon it became obvious to the regulars that I was not just another scuffler banging balls around. I had superior skills, and to get games I had to give up weight. The seven or eight ball in 9-Ball or perhaps 8-6 in One Pocket. The locals liked me because I was so accommodating in making games. I would ask them what they wanted, and usually that was what they got. I discovered that it wasn't hard to give up big weight in One Pocket. If I had a weak player I could give them just about anything, and still control the game.

Games like 10-5 and 8-4 became standard issue for me. The suckers loved it, thinking they had a real chance to win. So I would troll them along at $5 and $10 a game and always manage to eke out a small victory. Beating a guy out of twenty or thirty dollars was no big deal, and wouldn't scare them off. I developed a retinue of regular *customers*.

If you were making forty or fifty dollars a day back then, you were in the chips. I had a bank account with a healthy four figures in it, and a stash at home as well. I liked to start each day with a twenty dollar bill in my pocket and see what I could do with it. If I went home with fifty or sixty dollars at the end of the day, it had been a good day. My rent was $25 a week for a single apartment, and gas was thirty cents a gallon. You could eat well on $5 a day, no problem.

To my amazement, I soon discovered that I was better off than about 99% of the pool players I ran into. And I'm talking top players, the names of that era. Most of them couldn't get a game, because they were too good. They had to try to match up with each other, and that took backers to make it happen. I found myself loaning five and ten dollars to men who had been my heroes not so long ago. It put things into perspective for me. I was making money every day, while these guys were sitting on their butts, hoping for a live one to walk in. Weird huh?

CALIFORNIA DREAMING

My first trip to Long Beach took me to a wonderful spot called Beautiful Billiards, and it was! They lined up to play me, and pay me! I played one guy after another and finally met their champ, "Long Beach Dickey". He was a straight shooting young kid, but no match for me at *roll out* 9-Ball. I controlled the games and won something like $80 at five a game. I had fleeced Beautiful Billiards for the tidy sum of $150, and went home quite happy.

The next day I gleefully returned (as promised) to my new favorite poolroom. Dickey was no where to be found and neither were any of the other pigeons. One young guy confided in me that no one would play me now that I had beaten Dickey. But he told me where I could find another game. There was a place on Long Beach Blvd. named The Hole, and the owner's son was called "Trip". His dad would stake him to play nearly anyone who came in looking for a game. My new 'steerman' wanted to go along for the ride, and hopefully a cut of the action.

It was a short ride over to The Hole, but I wouldn't have even noticed it without my new partner giving me directions. Aptly named, The Hole was hidden away in the basement of an office building. We descended the stairs and entered a fairly large room, with maybe a dozen Gold Crowns. Not bad, I thought. And who is practicing Straight Pool on the front table? Why it was Trip, I was quietly informed. I sauntered over and watched him hit a few balls. He was running out the rack fairly easily, so I waited until he finished. As soon as the last ball was made, I asked him if he wanted a game. "Sure," he replied. "What do you play?"

I never asked anyone to play One Pocket, because that would almost definitely kill your action. Only seasoned players played One Hole, and it was a dead giveaway. But everyone played 9-Ball, so that was always my first choice. I replied to Trip, "How about some 9-Ball?" "Okay," he said, "how much?" "What do you like to play for?" was my response. "How about a 'race to eleven' for fifty dollars?" he said. Hey, this guy was a live one. I got a good steer here.

So I've been in this joint less than ten minutes, and I already have a fifty dollar game. I'm beginning to really like Long Beach. Trip turns out to be a decent enough player. He can run out, which is more than most of the guys I play with can do. So I have to go to my "A" game right away, which I would do for this size bet anyway. Once again, I love *push out* or *roll out*

9-Ball. To get *ball In hand* a player must commit two consecutive fouls. You can push out on any shot you don't like, and your opponent has the option to shoot, or pass it back to you. The better player has a huge advantage in this game.

Meanwhile back at the ranch, I get out to a small lead and I'm up about 7-4 when Trip is at the table running balls. All of a sudden he drops to the floor, and starts to twitch and make funny noises. I'm in a state of total shock. What the fuck is going on here? I haven't a clue. Several players in the room are just standing there, watching him go through his contortions. I'm thinking we should get help for him. I want to do something for this guy who is obviously in distress. But someone tells me to leave him alone. He'll be all right.

Sure enough, after a couple of minutes he seems to come to, and begins to rise to his feet. Trip looks around, sees his cue on the table, and starts to take it apart. I'm watching in astonishment. What is this guy doing? He puts his cue in the case and heads for the counter. Hold on one big second! I head him off, and ask him what he's doing. He looks at me like he has no idea who I am. I remind him we are playing for money. He looks surprised, and asks me what the game is. I tell him we are playing 9-Ball for $50. He then asks me the score. Wow! I could tell him anything, but I don't. I tell him I'm leading 7-4 going to eleven and he's shooting.

Trip calmly walks back to the table, takes out his cue, and goes back to work, like nothing had happened. What a shark! But he won't get me with this move. I bear down and win the set easily. He pays me off and thanks me for playing. Okay, but I don't even ask him to play anymore. I'm still in a state of semi shock from what I just saw minutes before. I quickly get the Hell out of there with my new buddy. I give him ten bucks for steering me, and ask him what that was all about. He tells me that Trip is an epileptic, and he just had a seizure. He said it happens all the time, and that I handled it quite well. Little did he know how shook up I was.

HUSTLING 60'S STYLE

There were many more experiences that stick out from those early years in sunny Cal. I got chased out of a bar in Gardena by a guy with a knife, over a $3 game of Eight Ball. I made a kick shot on the eight, and he decided that it was a bad shot, since I didn't call the rail as well as the eight ball. I was winning a few games at the time, and figured he was just trying to stiff me for the last game. I told him to just forget it. But he wanted me to pay him! And I refused. That's when I saw the knife, and the nasty look in his eye. I made a quick left out the door.

On a happier note I discovered the Santa Ana Playhouse, a huge night club in Orange County. They had four bar tables that were constantly in play all night long. The quarters were lined up along the rail, sometimes ten or twelve deep, and everyone was playing for something! It could be a dollar, but many games were for two or three dollars, and a few were for five. I put up my quarter and waited, and waited, and waited. Finally, after what seemed like eons, it was my turn. I made a determination that I was NOT going to the back of this line again.

I proceeded to win something like the next forty or fifty games in a row, until the place finally closed about 4 AM. My pockets were stuffed with bills, so many I had lost count. When I got home, and went through my ritual of unfolding each bill and putting it neatly in place (I still do this), I discovered I had won well over a hundred dollars. I was in hog heaven.

I returned the following Saturday night, and a group of locals greeted me warmly. It seems this was *their* spot, and they had allowed me one freebie. It was kind of like the surf wars that erupt occasionally along the coast, between local surfers and visitors. These guys let me know in no uncertain terms that this was their spot, and not mine. I had to leave or face the consequences, and I didn't want to know what they were. Bye bye Playhouse.

Next I hooked up with "Sunshine", real name Al Sunshine, an old time pool hustler from New York. He is mentioned in Fat's book, The Bank Shot and Other Great Robberies. Al is "the kid in the NYU sweater" who was hustling rooms all over New York, and pretending to be a college student. But that was a long time ago. Now Sunshine is an old timer hanging around Ye Billiard Den, trying to eke out a living. He saw me as a meal ticket.

Al proposed to take me on as my coach and backer. He will find me games, stake me to play, and split the winnings with me. I had never made this kind of arrangement before, preferring to go it alone for the most part. But Sunshine made it sound like a great proposition. He had some good spots for me, and he was putting up all the dough. So why not?

Off we went the next day, me driving and Sunshine giving directions. He showed me how to get to the Gardena Bowl, and put me in action against some Asian kid, who I quickly dismantled. Next we were off to Gage Bowl, and a little tougher game with a guy named Mike. It took me all day to relieve him of his cash, but with Sunshine coaching me I managed to make a score. It was late, and we had won over a hundred dollars. We were done for the day.

Day two took us to other rooms I had never been in before. The first was the Silver Cue in Huntington Park, where I played an excellent player named Jerry Vaughn. We broke even at 9-Ball, but he didn't fare as well at One Pocket. From there we went to Downey Family Billiards, and I dusted a couple more guys in there. Another day, another hundred to the good. Sunshine definitely knew the spots.

The next day it was more of the same, off to the Valley this time, and a few more out of the way spots. We won again and again. Al seemed to know just where to go for a player my speed. After four days we were winners over four hundred, and best of all, Sunshine was chopping the money with me every day. On the last day of our 'partnership', Al took me around the corner to the nearby room, Mothers. I had been there before and didn't do much. It was mostly populated by Jewish kids from the neighborhood. They weren't into throwing their money away to a hustler like me.

But Al had a plan. Mothers had two Snooker tables, and "Hollywood Jack" played in there daily. He was a known gambler, and a very good Snooker player. Al wanted me to play him. I told Al that I knew Jack, and didn't like my chances playing Snooker with him. 9-Ball no problem, even One Pocket I would play, but Snooker NO! He now informs me that I will play who and what he tells me to play. Well, okay, it was his money after all. So in comes Jack, and he sees me and walks right over. Before he can say a word, I ask him if he wants to play some 9-Ball. Jack smiles at me and says he has no chance against me at 9-Ball, but he would play me some Snooker for fifty a game.

Al says, "play the man." I once again remind Al this may not be such a good game for us. He growls at me, "Get out there and play!" So I did and four games later, after we're stuck two hundred, Al pulls me up. We walk outside, and Sunshine proceeds to ream me up and down, and tell me what a bum I am. It didn't matter that I won everywhere we went the prior four days. That was ancient history now. He was only concerned with my poor performance against Jack, and the loss we just took. I made a vow that day to never have another backer. And I haven't!

The late Richie Florence, a Southern California legend.

HEADING NORTH

I had done well in L.A. for about a year or so, when I decided a change of scenery would do me good. I had heard how beautiful Santa Barbara was, so I packed my stuff and took the short drive north. My first day there I visited the local pool room and got zero action. Depressing! But one of the locals told me about a bar spot where there were money games most every night. Promising!

I had a little dinner and hit the spot about 8 PM. Not much doing yet, so I banged the balls around to get the feel of the table. No sooner than I started to play, a guy at the bar asks me if I'm looking for a game. How accommodating. I said sure, I *love* to play. He tells me to wait a while, because the players will be in soon. And just like he said, about 9 PM a guy walks in and puts a quarter on the table while I'm shooting. Very cool!

His first words to me are, "How about some Eight Ball for five a game?" Okay, why not. I like Santa Barbara already. Five hours and three players later I am $140 richer, and the bar is closing. One of my opponents is a professor at a nearby college, another is a doctor, and I think an attorney got in the mix too. This was an upscale bar, with mostly professional people meeting and drinking in there. The money they lost that night seemed insignificant to them. But not to me!

I spent my first night in a motel, and rented a nice apartment the next day for $175 a month. I'm officially a resident of Santa Barbara! I continue to go into my new watering hole, but the action dries up within days. I just caught them on a lucky day the first time. I rarely see these same guys again, and when I do they only want to play for drinks. So it's time to branch out again. Near my apartment is a bowling alley with pool tables, and I find an occasional cheap game in there. A few miles up the road is UC Santa Barbara, and they have a poolroom right off campus, full of young guys from well-to-do families.

I begin making this drive nearly every day, and prospecting the college pool room. There are enough kids here that will play me $2 9-Ball (yes, I said two a game), that I can make my expenses, but that's about it. Somehow I am attracted here anyway. The pretty college girls and the nearby beaches may have had something to do with it. After one month in Santa Barbara, I move to Isla Vista and the campus of UC Santa Barbara. I am now living in an apartment one block from the ocean, and only two blocks from the pool room. I become a regular in Campus Cue, and make that my new home base. It's amazing to me that if you hang around a pool room for a week, you are now a *regular*. It happens that quick!

The professor I played in that bar a few weeks before teaches on this campus, and he is legendary in the pool room for playing in high stakes games. The stories abound of him losing hundreds of dollars playing Straight Pool. With him, I'll play Straight Pool, all day and all night. He becomes my goal and my target. Alas, I never get him. He proves just too elusive for me, skittering off when he sees me in the poolroom. Someone has knocked my action I'm sure, but what can I do. In the meantime I discover a late night poker game, populated by some of the more affluent students. I am invited to sit in and proceed to rob the game a few times, before my invitation is rescinded. The host quietly informs me that I must be a student at UC Santa Barbara to play in this game. New rule! The Helfert rule!

Not to worry, one of the poker players has told me about a topless bar on the outskirts of Santa Barbara, where he has seen high stakes pool being played. He gives me the low down on a guy called "DJ", who is the head of the local motorcycle gang. He is a big guy, mostly bald and has a peg leg; a peg leg just like Captain Hook. It turns out to be true. I venture down there on a Friday night with my buddy Bob Morris, who is the second best pool player around. It's a rough spot, full of bikers and assorted bad asses. The music is blasting, a girl is dancing topless, and DJ is holding court on the bar table.

We sit down at the bar, and watch him slaughter some poor schlep for twenty a game. He is ridiculing the guy, while he's winning game after game. My first thought is where do these guys get that kind of money, and my second thought is how do I get some. DJ beats the guy out of sixty or eighty dollars, while we're watching. He's not that good, just a straight shooter. His cue ball control is only fair, and he doesn't make any real hard shots. He prefers to just bang the balls in the hole. The poor guy he's beating on finally quits, and DJ takes a look around the bar. In a loud arrogant voice he proclaims, "Anybody in here want to play some for fifty a game?"

The place falls dead silent, except for me. I turn to Bob and say quietly, "He doesn't play good enough to play for fifty a game." DJ hears this remark and looks at me, "What did you say!" I am quiet now, acting scared. Once again, "TELL ME WHAT YOU JUST SAID!" Quietly, I tell him that he isn't good enough to play for fifty dollars. He throws a fifty dollar bill on the table and says, "Get up here and play big mouth!" Reluctantly, I get up and slowly walk to the table. I fish around in my pocket and find a hundred dollar bill, and show it to DJ. Okay, let's go he says and puts a quarter in the table. I am in a $50 game of Eight Ball with DJ, President of the local outlaw motorcycle gang. Scary, but exciting!

I'll never forget that first game. I was not about to lose for fifty bucks, and I ran out the first rack and ended up with a bank shot, cross side on the eight ball. I have to make it, otherwise he has an open table and can keep me tied up. I take my time, concentrate, and bank the eight right in the heart of the pocket. DJ throws fifty on the table and puts another quarter in the chute. Pretty soon we are playing for a hundred a game, the biggest pool game of my life. And DJ is throwing hundred dollar bills on the table, one after another. He does win a game once in a while, but I have his nose wide open. This big badass is going off big time. To me!

After a couple of hours, I have almost all of his money, maybe $1,600 or so. Now he wants to put up the title to his Harley parked outside against $1,000. We agree to play two out of three games for the bike, and I win that too. DJ is beaten and embarrassed in front of his gang. He looks at me with sinister eyes, and tells me he has $100 left, and he's going to fight me for it. I'm no coward, but DJ is twice my size. I tell him that I'm a pool player, not a fighter. He informs me that I'm not getting out of there with the money, unless I fight him.

I WILL NOT GIVE UP THE CASH! Period! If I have to fight to keep it, I will. I tell him that he can kick my ass if he has to, but I'm keeping the money I won. He motions for me to go out the back door with him. I follow him out, thinking of my best strategy. I make up my mind to go for his nuts, and bite him, and claw his eyes if I have too. I will go down fighting. My buddy Bob has a forlorn look on his face, like he's watching me walk to my death. We get outside, and DJ turns to me and reaches out his hand. Is this a trick? He looks me in the eyes and says, "I just wanted to see if you had the guts to come out here with me." Now he shakes my hand and walks back in the door. Whew, that's a relief!

Bob and I head to a nearby Denny's that's open all night. We sit down in the booth and I count the money. I give half to Bob, since we were partners. He is thrilled and tells me I can keep the bike. I have the title in my pocket and the bike is sitting back at the bar. DJ told me he will buy it back from me in a few days, and I should just leave it there. True to his word, DJ calls me in a couple of days and we arrange to meet at the bar, and he buys back the title for $1,000. This big bad outlaw has become a soft spoken gentleman. But that's not the end of the story.

A week or so later, on the front page of the Santa Barbara newspaper, is a story about the arrest of a notorious drug dealer, with his photo. The cops have raided DJ's home, and found tens of thousands of dollars in drugs, cash and weapons. He actually had a Thompson sub machine gun in his possession. Nice game I had huh?

I go to the pool room that day, and all the kids are talking about the big drug raid. It seems that some of them were his customers. DJ was well known around campus. Late in the afternoon, I head back to my apartment. When I get there the door is ajar, but I never leave my door unlocked. I walk in cautiously, and no one is there. I'm standing in the middle of the living room, when a guy emerges from behind the door. I'm scared shitless! He's in a suit and identifies himself as a detective from Santa Barbara. Another cop comes out of my bedroom. SHIT! One of them tells me to slowly put down the case I'm carrying. It's a pool cue I tell them, as I set it on the floor.

They frisk me and then ask me to sit down, and proceed to question me about my "relationship" with DJ. He had my phone number in his little black book, so they decided to pay me a visit. I come clean with them, telling them I'm a pool player and I'd been gambling with DJ. They ask me if I ever bought drugs from him, and I say no. One of the cops has found my little stash of weed in the bedroom, and he shows it to me. I tell them that I do smoke pot from time to time, and I gamble at pool, and if they want to arrest me for that, then go ahead. After a few more minutes they leave, telling me they may want to talk to me again, so I shouldn't leave town. I never heard from them again. Thank God!

A FEW SMALL RIOTS

Shortly after my game with DJ, the anti-war protests were heating up, especially on college campuses where the kids were now vehemently against the Viet Nam war. The campus of UC Santa Barbara was no different, and the kids seemed to focus their attention on the new branch of Bank of America being constructed off campus, about a block from *my* poolroom. They viewed this new construction as part of the "military-industrial" complex ruling America, as one of the young students was kind enough to explain to me.

Some of the students actually tried to block construction, holding signs aloft proclaiming the misdeeds of our government and Bank of America, and walking a picket line around the construction site. Then it got UGLY! Someone firebombed the new building at night and set it ablaze. Kids were milling around the fire in a celebratory mood, when police arrived and began confronting them. The situation deteriorated fast, and pretty soon kids were being cuffed and led away to police vans. A riot ensued with college kids throwing rocks and bottles at the police, and the cops chasing them down and beating them with billy clubs.

I witnessed the early stages of the riot from my perch, less than a block away in front of the pool room. You could see the fire, and hear the screaming and yelling going on everywhere. Kids were running in every direction, and the cops were pursuing them and arresting whoever they caught. I decided it was a good time to get back to the safety of my apartment. To get back there I had to circumvent the main riot area. It was bad, police all over in riot gear, and kids yelling at them and throwing things. The cops were being provoked and they reacted harshly. They would chase kids right into their apartments, and drag them away in handcuffs.

I made it home safe, little more than two blocks from the heart of the riot. I turned on the TV and watched the news. The newscasters were proclaiming that Isla Vista was now under "Marshall Law" by declaration of the Sheriff. It was being called the "Bank of America Riot". What I had witnessed was more of a police riot than anything. Once the police started arresting kids who were just watching the fire, that's when it erupted. And then the cops just went crazy, banging heads and administering beatings to anyone they could catch. It was scary!

I wanted to get the Hell outta Dodge. I packed up my car and tried to leave, but all the streets out were blocked off by police cruisers. They had cordoned off Isla Vista, no one was being let in and no one could leave. SHIT! I remembered a little used dirt road that led down to the beach. And you could drive along the dunes and there was another dirt road that led back to the highway a couple of miles from campus. I wondered if this road was blocked also. I checked it out and no one was there. I drove with my lights off until I reached the main road which led onto Highway 101 going north. I drove all the way to San Francisco that night!

I was never to return to Isla Vista. I left my furniture, bedding, pots and pans, plates and kitchen utensils etc. I didn't care. I had my clothes, my TV, my stereo and my cash! I could buy more furniture.

Ah, beautiful San Francisco, the City by the Bay. Freedom! I could go back to work. First stop, the fabled Cochran's Billiards and the Palace was right down the street. I spent my first week hanging around these two spacious rooms. Both were full of players and action. One problem, it was too much like New York. These rooms were full of good players. I found myself battling to make a few dollars each day. I played Ronnie Barber, Joe Smiley, Go away Jesse and some Bank Pool with Trees. This was tough action, not what I was looking for. Time to branch out once more.

I went over to Oakland first and found a "black" pool hall where One Pocket was the order of the day. I was the only white guy in the place, and the local hustlers greeted me with open arms. After I beat a couple of them for small money, I didn't feel quite so welcome anymore. I hit the road quick and drove down to Berkeley. There was one small pool room on the campus of Cal Berkeley called Kips. I set up shop there and did my best to fit in. Within days I knew all the regulars and they knew me. They thought I was a new student who liked to play pool. They were half right.

I was making money in Kips from day one, a $2 9-Ball game here (pay after $10 was my M.O.) and a $5 One Pocket game there (also pay after two games). In those days (the late 60's) you could survive just fine making twenty or thirty dollars a day. I was staying in a nearby hotel for $55 a week. I had developed a taste for college girls in Santa Barbara, and there were some cuties all over Berkeley. It was the 'hippie' days and free love was part of the scene. If you liked someone, sleeping together was acceptable. I liked it here, a friendly pool room, good weed and pretty girls. What more could a twenty four year old hustler ask for?

I was just getting settled in and beginning to look for an apartment, when the "war" once again intervened. Cal Berkeley was a campus full of activists, and the school newspaper published many of their anti war proclamations. Across the street from my hotel was a park, where several demonstrations had been held. It was called "Peoples Park," meaning it belonged to the *people* and not to authorities. One day the authorities decided to fence in Peoples Park. Their intentions were to pave it over and make a parking lot out of it. Except the *people/students* weren't going for it. They decided to tear down the newly constructed fence.

How did I know about all this? I was an eye witness to the whole thing, from the safety of my fourth floor window overlooking the park. I woke one morning to the sounds of screaming and yelling outside. I looked out my window, and saw hundreds of students surrounding the newly fenced-in park. The campus police would not let them inside the park. The kids were shaking the high fences and trying to bring them down. This went on for quite a while and finally the kids, through weight of numbers, began to knock down the fences on one side.

This brought on the police in riot gear, who waded into the crowd with batons flashing. They had on helmets and carried shields, and looked like storm troopers. They acted like them too, banging heads indiscriminately. If you were within range, you were going to get your lumps.

From my vantage point it was an ugly scene, like watching a movie but also being a part of it. I stayed in my room by the window for hours, a witness to all that was transpiring before me. The police were using tear gas to disperse the students, and it was working. They were running in all directions. I distinctly heard the sound of gunshots a couple of times too and I wondered where they were coming from. The next day I found out a student named James Rector was shot and killed by the police. He had been on a roof and was suspected of throwing rocks down at them. A couple of other students were injured by gunfire that day. "Kent State" was still a few years away. The Peoples Park Riot was its precursor.

When things seemed to calm down late in the day, I ventured out, heading to the pool room, where else. On the way there, I noticed the main streets were blocked off, and troops of riot police marched in formation up and down, eyeing the few scattered groups of students on the sidewalks. A couple of kids were shouting out epithets to the cops as they approached. Not a good idea I thought, and sure enough a couple of cops broke ranks and went after them. This led to more name calling, and suddenly the cops were in full battle mode. The ranks broke and cops ran everywhere chasing kids, batons flailing. Tear gas canisters were being shot into alcoves and business entrances on both sides of the street. There was no safe haven for me either.

I did what I do best in situations like this. I ran like a deer around the corner, and into the hallway leading to the pool room. Inside I felt safe, and everyone was talking excitedly about the events of the day. I told them that the cops were right around the corner, and firing tear gas at the kids. A couple of guys went outside to look, and no sooner had they opened the door then a canister flew into the hallway.

When these things go off, the whole area is immediately filled with gas. In those few moments before the front door could be shut, a small cloud of tear gas entered the pool room. We were all tearing up and covering our faces. Fortunately it was not a lot of gas and we were all okay fairly soon. But the noxious fumes hung in the air for a long time, and made it uncomfortable inside the pool room.

It was a lot more uncomfortable to be outside though, so we hung in the pool room until it closed at 2 AM, and then slowly filtered out to the mean streets of Berkeley. Things had quieted down, and there was virtually no one on the streets, except for a police car on nearly every corner. I walked alone back to my hotel, packed my stuff and left that night for Southern Cal. This was becoming a pattern for me, and I was feeling a little traumatized by what I had seen in the last few months. I never saw another riot except on television, but I will never forget those terrible days in 1969 and early 1970.

In hindsight I realize now my sequence of events is backward. I visited San Francisco first, experienced the Peoples Park Riots, and escaped to Santa Barbara, where I witnessed the police riot on campus. From Isla Vista I headed south back to L.A. That's what happens when you are relying on nearly forty year old memories. But trust me when I tell you I was there, and got gassed in Berkeley and watched the Bank of America burn in Isla Vista. Maybe I'm suffering from some lingering post traumatic stress syndrome.

A FEW OTHER BIG SCORES

Back in the safe and sunny climes of Southern Cal, I once again returned to my home base at Ye Billiard Den in Hollywood. It was easy to settle back into my old ways, schmoozing with the locals, giving up weight and making a living the old fashioned way. Winning it!

One day a young kid from San Diego showed up and was looking for a game. I was always ready to take on a newbie, and we played some $5 9-Ball for a few hours with no real conclusion, other than I knew he shot awfully straight. He said he was on leave from the naval base down there, and everyone in San Diego knew him as "Navy Gary". He'd heard there was some good bar table action in L.A., and that's what he was looking for. He had a pocket full of money, so okay why not.

That night we headed off to Daisy Mae's in Orange County, the hottest bar spot around. All the Mexican champions hung out in there, and they attracted many hustlers trying to take them off. I told Gary to avoid the Mexicans. Guys like Sergio, Mario and "Little Al" were too good. There were other likely candidates for us to do battle with. And we found a good one right away.

When we got there, "Charlie The Ape" was holding court on one of the tables, betting high with one of the Mexicans. He was getting weight, something like the seven and the break. Charlie broke like Godzilla, making two and three balls nearly every time. After a while the game came to a close, with Charlie taking down the cash. Gary immediately asked Charlie to play, a very bold move for a newcomer to Daisy Mae's. But Navy Gary was fearless, I was soon to find out.

Charlie wanted to know who this kid was. Gary told him he was a sailor on leave from San Diego, the truth. He even told Charlie what boat he was stationed on. This seemed to pique Charlie's interest, and he began some friendly chatter with Gary. Pretty soon the chat got around to playing pool for money, and Charlie saw that Gary was serious. Soon enough they were playing $20 Eight Ball, not a bad game to start out with.

Gary started right out rifling balls in from everywhere, and beating on Charlie. Pretty soon he was $100 winners, and Charlie wanted to raise the bet. No problem, jack it up to $40 a game. Within a couple of hours they were playing $100 a game. When Gary got him stuck around a thousand Charlie quit. Charlie was hot when he realized how good this kid could play.

He began asking Gary to give him a better game, and Gary kept refusing to give him any spot. I was quite content to take the thousand and leave. But not Gary. He whispered in my ear, "Watch this."

Gary tells Charlie, "Okay, you've got the eight ball, I just want to keep playing." That's all Charlie wanted to hear, and he literally jumped to his feet. You have to realize Charlie played in this joint almost every day, and was a very strong player. No matter, Gary was not missing anything that night, and after a few hours he had Charlie dead broke. We were winners something like $2,400. Charlie was seething mad now, and said he would put up the title to his car against $400. It was an older Chevy Nova. Don't ask me why, but Gary played him and won the car too.

This is when the real problems began. Charlie grabbed the title back from the bartender and told us to get fucked, he wasn't paying. Gary wanted the title and I wanted to get out of there. I had my little .25 in my back pocket, but it didn't seem like enough gun for this gorilla. It might just make him madder if he got shot. Charlie was ranting and raving, and actually picked up the end of the bar table with one hand just to scare us. It scared me! Gary told me to get the car and pull it around front, and keep the motor running. He would stay there and deal with this lunatic.

Gary kept Charlie busy while I snuck out the back door. I quickly pulled my 'Vette around the front of the bar and next thing I know Gary comes dashing out, jumps in and yells, "Let's go!" I gun it and roar off just as Charlie comes charging out the door, waving his fists in the air. Gary is laughing his ass off. He thinks this is all funnier than Hell. I don't share his humor at that moment. Gary says he told Charlie he was going to the bathroom, and would be back to play him some more.

He offered to play Charlie a second time for the car, and Charlie went for it. That's when he made his mad dash out the door on the way to the restroom.

We made it home just fine, and chopped up gobs of Charlie's ill gotten drug money. Gary went back to San Diego shortly after that, and I didn't see him again for a very long time. After his Navy stint was over he returned home to Kansas City, where he married and went into the hair salon business with his wife Zona (her real name). He continued playing pool and became known as "The Munch" around there. Where that name comes from I have no idea. What I do know is that Gary and Benny Conway were the two best players in Kansas City for years.

One other time I became a steer man and made a telephone number score, although it was to prove costly afterwards. Let me tell you about it. There was a young player out of Cincinnati named Frank Tullos, who I met when we were kids in Mergards. He was in college and decided to fly out to California on his Winter break. Naturally he calls his old pool room buddy Jay. I meet up with him and he tells me he is playing the best pool of his life right now, and he wants to play some good players.

I took him down to Tournament Billiards and he matches up with Cecil Tugwell, one of the top black players in L.A. I didn't really like Frank's chances here, but he surprised me and beat Cecil playing 9-Ball. Frank refused to play Cecil One Pocket. Good move! Frank asks me where the best players hang out. I told him Richie Florence is hanging out around the Tropicana Bowl, but he can't beat Richie. No one can! And there are better games for him anyway. I tell Frank about a place called Five Points in El Monte that is full of hustlers, and some are excellent players. He wants to go that night.

Off we go to El Monte, forty five minutes and a world away from Hollywood. It's a blue collar, pick-up truck kind of town, and the pool rooms are gritty little places full of hustlers and assorted scum bags. Five Points has the best of them, all under one roof. Pool hustlers, card sharps, short money artists and other scammers all reside here between 'jobs'. I decided to take my friend Leon along with us. Leon was a confessed bank robber, who always carried a .45 neatly tucked in his pants. He had already helped me collect one debt from a gambler who had refused to pay up. Leon just lifted his shirt to reveal the gun, and the guy coughed up the dough quick. Turns out it was a good thing we brought Leon along.

We walk into a poolroom full of top players. It just so happens Mike Massey, Larry Lisciotti and others are assembled at Five Points during this time frame. The pool world equivalent to New Yorkers spending their winters in Florida. All are under the tutelage and in the stable of one John Miller, aka "Popcorn". He arranges games for them, and teaches them various new ways to make a buck in the poolroom. Scams and con games being his specialties. Popcorn is a mover and shaker of some renown in the West Coast pool firmament. Players flock to him like lemmings to the sea.

But Frank is unconcerned about all this. He just wants to play, anyone and everyone. He is in dead punch and has no fear of anybody. First he pounds "Philly Joe" Veasey who quickly withdraws, and then Mike Massey steps up and the game is back on. I know all these guys, and try to clue Frank in. He

45

just smiles and shrugs his shoulders. He really doesn't care about reputations or credentials. He is bubbling with confidence, and for good reason. Frank is in "no miss" mode. He beats Mike out of about $100 at ten a game, and he pulls up too. Now Larry Lisciotti wants a piece of Frank. I figure this is the end of the road for Frank. Larry is one of the premier young players in the country at that time. He had hustled me out of $200 playing One Pocket a couple of months prior, after Popcorn had sent him to *visit* me.

They also start off for ten a game, but shortly the bet elevates to $20. Larry goes for around $200, before he also hits the rack. The whole room is stirring now, two of the top hustlers have been beaten. Now it's time to bring in the big gun, Eddie "The Hat" Burton. Eddie Burton was a known killer and played maybe the eight ball under Richie Florence. I told Frank we could quit winners now. After all we had already made over $300 that night, a nice score back then. Frank would have none of it. He agreed to play Burton a $600 freeze-out. Six ahead for the $600. This was a serious game, circa 1970.

The first set lasted several hours and finally Frank took it down. We were now $900 to the good. I was thrilled and figured that was it. But Popcorn didn't see it that way. He wanted Frank to play another $600 set. Frank readily agreed. It was after midnight when the set started, and Eddie was gobbling pills and his eyes were as wide as headlights. Frank was playing on the *natch*, but he was young, healthy and strong. He had no quit in him. The second set may have lasted two or three hours and Frank took it off again. Everyone in the pool room seemed a little frantic. No one had come in there and taken off Five Points before. But Frank was doing just that.

I have to say these matches were as good as I'd seen 9-Ball played up till that time. Both these guys were making everything from everywhere. They were running out rack after rack. But Eddie would occasionally blunder on his position and have to push out. He was a little too *hyped* up, and he would push out for extremely difficult shots. Frank would let him shoot, and he would often miss these long rail banks or very thin cuts. Then Frank would take advantage and run out the rack. Little by little Frank wore Eddie down, to where he looked like a beaten dog when it was over. Frank ended up winning five sets that night, for a $3,000+ score.

Frank Tullos had completely cleaned out Five Points, and all the hustlers in there. And I was the one who brought him. After the dust settled it was like a morgue in Five Points. There was complete silence as we exited the room, and went next door to the all night coffee shop to cut up the money. I think we gave Leon 10% for protecting us. No telling what might have happened if he hadn't been there. Leon had those cold steel eyes that gave people the shivers when he looked at them. And if you looked closely you could see the tell tale bulge under his shirt.

But this was not the end of the story. Frank took his winnings and flew back home to Cincinnati, and I stayed in Los Angeles and continued to ply my trade. A couple of weeks later I got a call at the poolroom from Popcorn. He seemed quite relaxed as we talked briefly about the game and how well Frank had played. I figured it was over and done with. How wrong I was. Popcorn inquired as to whether I would be interested in continuing our ongoing battle at One Pocket and Banks. We had played several times for ten and twenty a game, and it was a close match between us. I had a pocketful of his money, so I said sure. He invited me to come back out to Five Points and play, and I agreed. BIG MISTAKE!

The next night I drove back out to Five Points, alone! The first person I see when I walk in is Popcorn, banging balls around on a middle table. I walk over and he is friendly as can be. The big game from a few weeks past seems to be forgotten. We agree to play a little $20 One Pocket, and flip for the break. He wins and breaks the balls. It's my shot, and as I get down to shoot all the lights in the entire poolroom go out. It's pitch black in there. Before I can even think about what was happening, someone punches me, HARD! And then I'm getting hit from all directions, by more than one person. I'm on the ground and getting really worked over; kicked and punched over and over again. I have to fight back as best I can. I begin to bite, claw and scratch. I'm in total survival mode. Anything I can grab is going to be bitten hard, to the bone if possible. If I can grab someone's face, I go for the eyes trying to claw them out.

This battle rages on for maybe a minute or two, but it seems like an eternity. Suddenly it's over. No one is hitting me anymore. There is no one to grab. I sit on the floor, a wounded animal. Then the lights come back on. I see the whole crew from Five Points, lined up along the wall. They are staring back at me. I notice a few guys whose clothes are ripped and torn. They are bleeding too, just like me. I'm full of blood, but I don't feel anything but rage. Slowly I get to my feet. No one is saying a word, just looking at me. I must look horrible, mangled, torn to shreds. I gather my cue and case, and walk out the door. Not a word is spoken. Not by me or by them. Popcorn has a smile on his face; I notice that. Now it's over!

They have paid me back for bringing Frank Tullos to Five Points and busting the joint.

The epilogue to this story is that it was a few years before I saw Popcorn again. I walked up to him, and asked him point blank what that beating was all about. I'll never forget his reply to me. "These things happen in pool rooms," he smirked.

"Navy Gary" Serville

Frank Tullos

ODDS AND ENDS

Before I move on there are a couple of other stories that you might find interesting, that happened during this same time frame. My home room, Ye Billiard Den, is where I mostly hung around, and made plans where to go to find some action. In there I had quite a few regulars that would come in from time to time, and make donations to my favorite charity, me! One was Jack Ackerman, who was the composer and arranger for Judy Garland, and toured with her on concert tours. He loved to play 9-Ball and I was his favorite foe. I would give Jack the eight and the break, and we would play $50 sets. He was an outrageous character who loved to act up during our games. Everyone in the poolroom knew Jack was there, and he was an attention whore to say the least.

I had to fade his shenanigans every time we played, and it was probably why many other guys didn't want anything to do with him. I didn't mind playing second fiddle to Jack, as long as he paid me off after every set. And he always did faithfully. Jack was good for fifty to hundred every time I saw him, so he was all right in my book. Then we would go outside and cruise around in his Caddy smoking primo weed. Jack wasn't hard to like. A little tougher game was with "Crazy Bruce", and he was certifiable.

Before I deflower Bruce, I'll mention a couple of other regulars on my Hollywood dance card. "John The Dancer" was part of a well known dance team with his wife, and they even appeared on the Ed Sullivan Show. He got the eight ball whenever he wanted it. We would play fifty or hundred dollar sets, usually a short race, because he was always in a hurry to get somewhere. Only if he won the first set, would he stay and play one more. So it was a one barrel deal with him nearly every time. And if I lost the first set, I knew I was playing to get even, that's all.

Jimmy Caan was yet to become a well known actor, and he hung around The Den between gigs. He got the seven ball and was usually good for fifty or sixty bucks, at ten a game. I once beat him for two hundred, and he didn't come around for a couple of months. I was more careful after that. Once he made *Brian's Song*, a celebrated TV movie, we rarely saw him again. He was working all the time.

One other guy who was very popular with me and all the scufflers was Rudy Oliver, a high line pimp, who had a flock of gorgeous girls working for him. Rudy loved to play pool, and fancied himself a One Pocket player. In truth he didn't play too bad. The problem with Rudy was that he wanted to bet too high for most of the shortstops like me. I was uncomfortable playing for $100 a game back then. He wasn't a sucker and knew how to match up. One night he came after me, teasing me about playing. He asked me what I thought I could give him. I told him I felt like 8-6 was a fair game between us. That was it, he practically begged me to play.

I truly felt like I could give him that weight, but like I said, he wanted to bet a minimum of a hundred a game. I went home that night and lay in bed and had a talk with myself. I said, "Self, if you are ever going to move up to the next level you have to be willing to bet more money." In my heart, I knew I was a much better player than Rudy. My mistake was offering him a fair game. I should have said 8-7, but it was too late now. If I was going to beat him, it had to be at 8-6.

I went looking for Rudy the next night and found him at Celebrity Billiards. We hooked it up for $100 a game and the whole joint packed in to sweat it. At closing time, I had won $800, a lot of money for me back then. Rudy brushed it off like it was no big deal, but he never played me again. I felt like I had crossed a threshold. I was playing $100 a game pool now. Big action in those days. Okay, now let me tell you about Crazy Bruce.

Bruce was a good player himself, originally out of Miami, Florida, and on an extended road trip to Los Angeles. His favorite game was Eight Ball and he was tough action, but once he started going off he was done. If you could fade his tantrums you might book a score. Bruce was a handsome man, but had a masochistic bent. If he missed a ball he would berate himself loudly, tearing at his face and hair in an attempt to wound himself. He might put scratches on his face or tear clumps out of his hair. To say his antics were distracting and disturbing is putting it mildly. It was not easy concentrating on your own game, when your opponent was slightly nuts. I played Bruce several times, and would tell him at the start if he couldn't control himself I would quit. He would always agree, but once he got behind the flagellation would begin.

The last time we played was the most memorable. Bruce somehow kept it together for an entire session with me, satisfied to mutter profanities under his breath when things weren't going well for his side. Eventually he quit, after blowing a small sum to me. He asked me pleasantly enough if I was going to pay the time, and I said sure. While I was at the counter Bruce slipped out a side door, and walked to the parking lot alongside the poolroom. A moment later I heard a loud CLUNK outside. I wondered what had happened, so I peered out the side door and Bruce was laying on the ground in a heap. A couple of girls were standing there with their mouths wide open. I asked them what happened to him, and they told me he had stood in the middle of the parking lot, lowered his head and ran full speed into the wall head first, knocking himself out cold. Bruce was a strange egg all right.

Another high light of my days at Ye Billiard Den was my match with Willie Mosconi. He was on tour, and the room owner picked me to be his opponent. Pancho wanted the assignment, but Willie knew Pancho and didn't want to play a "hustler", which Pancho assuredly was. I was unknown to Willie at the time and that was a good thing. When I got the call I began practicing Straight Pool, a game I normally never played. I could run two to three racks fairly consistently on shooting ability alone, but a run over 50 was a rarity for me, with the lone 72 being my high run. I just did not play this game well; It was my weakest game. So I was very nervous when the big day arrived.

The place was packed to see the great Willie Mosconi slaughter Toupee Jay, as I was widely known back then. Willie played to the crowd, holding court for maybe thirty minutes before our match, shooting trick shots and making sure everyone knew how great he was. Now it was my turn and I was a wreck. I had to go out there and make a fool of myself. Willie purposely lost the lag and laid a good safe down on me. A ball was sticking out, and I had the corner pocket to shoot at. I could cut this ball in, and the cue ball would come off the end rail into the pack, and break it up. If I was playing 9-Ball with a sucker I'd never miss this shot. But right then I couldn't see or hear anything. It was like I was struck dumb for a moment.

I somehow mustered the courage to shoot, and fired away. The cue ball sped down the table and barely nicked the edge of the object ball. I had missed horribly! The crowd sat stunned by my feeble attempt and Pancho yelled out, "He hit it!" The room erupted in laughter at my ineptitude. I was humiliated and wanted to crawl under the table. No such luck. I had to sit there and watch Willie run rack after rack. He was nice enough to give me two or three more turns at the table, after he opened with a 119 ball run. I may have accumulated fifteen balls or so, before he mercifully ended the most embarrassing day of my life. I had forgotten how to play pool that day. I felt like a rank beginner.

On a brighter note is the way I chanced to earn the nickname which I initially hated, Toupee Jay. I had been prematurely balding since the age of nineteen, and was very uncomfortable with my receding hairline. I didn't want to look old at twenty three, so I found a wig maker in Hollywood who made me a very nice toupee. I was pleasantly surprised that when I ventured out to some old haunts looking for action, guys who I'd played before didn't recognize me. Or at least they weren't sure if I was the same guy they'd played a year or two before. More than once an opponent looked at me and said, "I know you from somewhere," and I would reply that he must have me confused with someone else. The toupee disguise worked well for a while until I tried this trick at Ye Billiard Den and was spotted by "Arizona Sean", who was one sharp cookie. He took one look at me and bleated out, "Why look who's here, it's Toupee Jay!" From that day on I had a new nickname, like it or not.

Sean was an excellent player, and had won the Arizona State Championship at age fifteen! He became very friendly with a handsome young man named Don Johnson, who used to hang around the Den with his gorgeous young girlfriend Melanie Griffith. This was before fame and fortune embraced them both. As far as I know Sean and Don remain friends to this day. What I do know is that Sean worked as a writer on scripts for Miami Vice, Don's hit television show. Sean and me got back together in the 1980's, to write the opening scene for *Harley Davidson and The Marlboro Man*. It was a pool scene in a bar, and Don played with a cue I gave him. I never did get that cue back.

But I digress. Sean had won a qualifier at Ye Billiard Den, that awarded him an entry into Fred Whalen's version of The World Pool Championships, held in 1971 at the Elks Lodge near downtown Los Angeles. I was introduced to Fred and he asked me to referee at the Straight Pool event, for five dollars a match. Sure why not, since I also got a free pass to get in and sweat all the great players. And I could see how my friend Sean fared against the champions. While I wasn't refereeing I was hanging around the practice room, listening to all the gab and discovering who the gamblers were among the Straight Pool crowd. Jimmy Moore was definitely one of them. He was constantly maneuvering for games and one night he got a good one.

A Snooker player from Canada was in the house watching Jimmy play. Someone mentioned to him that Jimmy played Snooker too, so after the match this guy challenges Jimmy to play some full rack Snooker for $50 a game. A pretty healthy bet back then, and Jimmy accepted his offer. Word got around and a bunch of us raced over to the nearby billiard room, where this snooker battle was going to take place. In those days many pool rooms still had a snooker table or two. I was in the forefront of the charge. When the game got underway, the walls were lined with sweaters.

I was sitting back in a comfy chair, looking forward to seeing some great Snooker being played, when I was approached by a young man I vaguely recognized. He asked me if I wasn't the referee he saw working the matches at the tournament. I told him yes, that was me. He then asked if I played pool. Hmmm, this conversation was getting interesting. I told him I played a little, but not Straight Pool. How about 9-Ball he asked? Sweet! I said sure, I play 9-Ball, what about you? A minute or two later we were on the next table playing $5 9-Ball. The Snooker game ceased to be important to me.

The kid could play, he probably fancied himself a local hustler of sorts. But he wasn't my speed, and I began collecting ten dollar bills from my new *friend.* We were paying off after two games, and he was stuffing a ten spot in the corner every time he lost. All the sweaters were watching Jimmy go at it, and no one was paying attention to my little game. That was fine with me. Suddenly all Hell broke loose in the poolroom. A crowd of men burst through the front door yelling it was a raid, and they were the police. Some were in uniform and some wore plain clothes. I couldn't believe what was happening. This bunch of cops went right back to the table where Jimmy was playing. Someone had tipped them off.

They quickly arrested Jimmy and the other guy, and handcuffed them both. Two plain clothes cops had been in the audience watching the game all along. Now one of them looked over at me and my opponent. He said we had been gambling too, and reached into the corner pocket and fished out a ten dollar bill. My heart sank. Briefly the cops debated what to do with us. The Captain finally decided that if the plain clothes guys saw us gambling, then we had to be arrested as well. And we were. My sweet game was over and I was going to jail. We were also handcuffed and led outside.

On the sidewalk, the guy I had been playing started getting mouthy with the cops. Bad move! They threw us both into the back of a police car, and prepared to take us to the police station for booking. This idiot sitting next to me in handcuffs wouldn't shut up. I could see the cops were getting irritated. I told the kid to please be quiet; it wasn't doing us any good. Two big cops were in the front seat, and without warning, the one in the passenger seat turned around and whacked the kid in the face. Hard! It scared the living shit out of me. I was sitting right next to him, and now the kid had a bloody nose. He did shut up though. That is until we reached the police station.

They lined us up; the four of us who had been arrested, and told us to sit on the bench and keep our mouths shut. Jimmy reassured me it was no big deal. We would have to post bail and they would let us go. I wasn't so sure though. Now the kid starts yammering away again like some kind of tough guy. The same cop saunters over, picks him up and slams his face against the wall. "I thought I told you to shut up," he says. Bloody nose number two! They took the kid away and threw him in the drunk tank. I found out later they kept him there all weekend. As for us, we sat on that bench for an hour or so, and then they asked us if we had money to post bail. The bail amount was $52. I'll never forget that number.

All three of us had the money, and we were taken one at a time to the counter, finger printed, photographed and relieved of $52. We signed some paperwork regarding an impending court date, and we were then released. Outside, Jimmy told me to forget about the court date. If you don't show up he told me, the money is forfeited and the case is over. Oh and one more thing, you will now have a misdemeanor police record for gambling. He made it sound like a badge of honor for pool players. So now you know, I have a gambling conviction on my record.

"Cowboy" Jimmy Moore

LIVING LARGE IN BAKERSFIELD

By 1969 I was pretty pumped up, with a healthy four figure bank account. Plus a couple of thou I kept around the house. My brother Bruce re-entered my life, making a decision to do his internship at Kern Medical Center in Bakersfield, California. I went up to visit him and naturally check out the local pool scene. There were several rooms in Bakersfield, with the largest being The Cue Ball in the heart of the downtown district. There was also a very active bar scene, with lots of low level action, perfect for me.

I helped Bruce move into his new pad, and stayed with him for a week or so. He quickly made friends with a cute nurse (grass didn't grow under his feet) and she became a regular visitor to *our* home. One day while Bruce was at work, a very pretty girl came to the door. Turns out Bruce had sent her over to help me unpack some of his stuff. Julie was her name, and she was best friends with his girlfriend Barbara. She was a nurse also. I was instantly smitten. You have to remember I hadn't had a girlfriend in years. Pool had been my only mistress.

Julie and I hit it off right away, and within a couple of months I had relocated to Bakersfield. I was living with Bruce, playing with Julie, and shooting pool when they were both busy, which was a lot of the time. I had no job or prospects for one. I was a pool player, plain and simple, and made no bones about it. I let Julie know in no uncertain terms I was not a working stiff. She didn't care, she was in love with me too.

I played all over Bakersfield, and played everyone who could play. Within a month or two I had a rep. I felt like I was the best player in town on big tables. I had already beaten Nate, the heretofore best player around. The bar action was non stop though. I could always find a game somewhere. Over in nearby Oildale, the rednecks who worked the oil fields had money and loved to gamble. I eventually worked my way up their pecking order, until I got matched me up with JD Tyner. JD owned a rigging company that set up oil wells. He had big money and liked to play high. He was the one they called when a road man came into town.

I met JD one night at Trouts, a notorious redneck bar in the heart of Oildale. Like I said, I would go anywhere and play anyone back then. We started out at $20 a game Eight Ball and worked up to $40 a game within an hour or so. JD could play! He was no DJ, the mark I beat in Santa Barbara. We traded run outs for a while but eventually I began to get the best of him. It seemed like everyone in the bar was betting on our match, and more than a few guys were taking a dislike to me. The bartender, Johnny Ingram, had seen me play and was betting more than I was. He was betting with three or four guys each game, ten and twenty a pop.

One particularly big guy began to give me a very hard time, and to his credit, JD tried to calm him down with no luck. That's when Johnny Ingram stepped in. He came out from behind the bar and told the guy to shut up when I was shooting, or he would personally throw him out. Now John wasn't much bigger than me, but this big guy calmed right down. I realized that Johnny Ingram was no one to mess with, and I was very glad he was on my side. I ended up a few hundred winners, and John must have won twice as much as me. He gave me a $100 bill and told me, "good shooting." We remained friends throughout my years in Bakersfield, and Johnny would call me whenever he ran into someone who was looking for a game.

Meanwhile Bruce got back into his racing hobby, and was busy building a Corvette in his spare time. I helped him out whenever he needed me. When the car was together, we tested it on the not yet open Highway 5. I remember towing it out there on a Sunday, when the crews were off work. We had this huge wide open highway to ourselves. No one was around, and there was no Highway Patrol to worry about. Bruce and I ran that 'Vette up and down that road at well over 100 mph.

After a few more tests we began racing at Riverside Raceway, Willow Springs and Laguna Seca. Bruce got his SCCA license, and soon after so did I. He was driving in the "National" competitions and I was driving in the "Regionals". Bruce had succeeded in getting me out of the poolrooms, which may have been his goal. By now Julie and I were married, and already had one little one. That's when tragedy struck, and Bruce was killed in the race at Phoenix International Raceway. I was lost! Completely! And my family was devastated. My mother and father never really got over Bruce's death. He was one of life's stars.

Bruce had just been accepted into NASA's training program for new astronauts. He was planning to move to Houston in the near future. Bruce had the *right stuff*. He was a trained physician with an engineering background, and he was only 5'8" and about 160 pounds. They looked for smaller men back then. All for naught though, Bruce was gone and I had lost my anchor. I found out that Bruce had named me on a $15,000 Life Insurance policy, and a check was sent to me within a couple of weeks. I had no clue what to do with my life now, until Julie's dad intervened.

John Gillett, her father, was a prominent businessman in Bakersfield, with a sand and gravel business. He found out that the Cue Ball was for sale, and the owners were men he knew. John introduced me to John Boydston and P.K. Nicholas, and we sat down and talked turkey. Didn't take me too long to figure out that they were tired of owning a pool room. Boydston was a realtor and Nicholas was an accountant. The Cue Ball had become a headache for them. I bought it for $40,000, $10,000 down with $600 a month payments, plus $700 a month in rent on the building. Naturally they owned the building too. These were savvy businessmen I was dealing with here. I had a five year lease with an option for five more at $750 a month rent.

The business was going nowhere when I took it over, barely paying the bills. I changed all that though. What I had going for me was an extensive knowledge of the poolroom business, acquired from observing many successful ones in operation. I saw many things they had been doing wrong at the Cue Ball. They had turnstiles you had to walk through to get in, like at a train station. Very unfriendly! And there were large signs all over telling you what the *rules* were. Also very unfriendly! The first thing I did was remove the turnstiles, and take down the rules. I basically had four *unwritten* rules. No drinks or cigarettes on the rails, no sitting on the tables, no fighting and no sleeping. The Cue Ball wasn't a motel!

I hired a couple of pretty girls to work the counter, and put my brother's '23 T Roadster on display in the front window. Bakersfield was a car crazy town, and everyone who was driving down the main drag, Chester Avenue, could gaze at this super cool car. It was Car Craft magazine's "Project Car of the Year" in 1967, before Bruce bought it. It definitely attracted attention! And the kids began rolling in. I had no alcohol and any kid fourteen or older could play pool at the Cue Ball. Within a few weeks the Cue Ball had become the hangout for all the high school and college kids in Bakersfield. With seven high schools plus Bakersfield College, that was a lot of kids. We were busy every day after school let out, and on the weekends it was packed. Mobbed might be a better word!

The Cue Ball had twenty two tables in 7,000 square feet of space. Plus we had a small arcade with sixteen machines, and a newly built dining area with seating for about fifty people total. The counter would seat maybe fifteen people, and I put in four large picnic tables and benches, to accommodate about thirty to thirty five more. The listed capacity for the room was 199 people, but we often had more than that on the weekends. The Fire Marshalls would sometimes make us stop letting people in, and threatened to shut me down on more than one occasion. I would frequently have a waiting list for pool tables with a dozen or more names on it, and the kids would hang out for hours to get a table.

Out front the sidewalks were very wide, and crowds of kids hung out there as well, waiting to be let in. On the street cars were continually cruising around the block, with the occupants engaged in loud exchanges with the kids who were standing around outside. I had to rent an additional parking lot at night from the neighboring shoe store to handle all the cars. The Cue Ball was some crazy scene and I was right in the middle of it, dispensing pool balls and cokes all night long, and trying to keep some order out of the madness.

Pool time was ninety cents an hour, with thirty cents extra for the third and fourth players. So the maximum per table was $1.50 an hour. Weekdays we might do $100-150 a day in pool time, and on weekends it might be double or triple that. Our food and drink business would usually be about the same. We sold hot dogs, hamburgers, sandwiches and pizza. A very good day was $500-$700 in total sales, with the occasional thousand dollar day (usually a holiday). I also had the revenue from the arcade and juke box (50-50 split with the vendor), and I had other machines dispensing peanuts, candy and cigarettes. The Cue Ball might do twelve thousand or more per month in business, but over half of that was clear profit. I was a rich man in terms of 1970's dollars.

After one year I bought a house in the Panorama Heights neighborhood, a ritzy section of town. I paid $24,000 for that house in 1973. My payments were a little over $125 a month. How things have changed! That house today would have to be worth several hundred thou, even in this depressed market. By now Julie and me had two young girls, and I was working seven days a week, raking in the dough. I would come home after two in the morning and sleep until nine or ten. Then I'd get up, have breakfast, and head out to buy supplies, before we opened at Noon. Normally I would come home for dinner, and one of Julie's wonderful meals, and then I was back off to work until the wee hours. Needless to say this took a toll on our marriage.

While all this was going on, I was still trying to be a pool player. From time to time players would come in looking for action, and naturally I would try to accommodate them. I'd make them play on the front table, so I could go behind the counter when necessary. This way I could take care of the business and play pool too. Bad idea! It took me about six months to realize that trying to play pool and work at the same time was just too difficult. I was getting beat pretty often. Later on I found out that my pool room (and me) was on every road man's list of places to visit.

Finally it dawned on me to try a new strategy. When a player came in looking for a game, I would tell him to come back at 2 AM when we were closing. That way I could close up shop and play pool in peace and quiet. It might just be me and a buddy or two and the player and his partner. We had the whole pool room to ourselves. I loved the atmosphere of the poolroom when it was empty. What had been a struggle for me before was now a pleasure. I had many late night games and did much better than before, making quite a few tidy scores. My *visitors* included Jimmy Marino, Hawaiian Brian, Larry Lisciotti, Wade Crane, Cuban Joe, Denny Searcy, Cole Dixon, Gabby, Billy Ray, Keith, Peter Gunn, Waterdog, Bakersfield Bobby and dozens of players you never heard of. Like Artesia Kenny, Jeff Mervis, The Wino, Jim Williams, Dan Boone, Tony Banks, Jerry Mackey, Billy Teeters, Little Lavita, Trucker John and some whose names I either didn't know or have forgotten. I may have played a hundred different guys in my years at The Cue Ball.

A memorable game was my first encounter with Billy Johnson (aka Wade Crane), who was accompanied by "Cuban Joe". I knew Joe from before and we had played One Pocket and Banks, with me getting slightly the best of it. Joe and I got into a *friendly* little $20 One Pocket game, while Billy sat on the rail and handled the money. The conversation between them led me to believe that Billy was his backer, and Joe played up how rich Billy was. After losing a few games to me Joe pulled up. He seemed pretty jovial considering I had just beaten him out of a few bucks.

He cozied up to me at the counter, and told me that his friend Billy was quite wealthy and loved to play 9-Ball for big money. I asked him how much, and he told me Billy liked to play for $50 or a $100 a game. That was big money back then, but Joe laid it down good and pretty soon Billy and I were in action. He stalled with me a little and I was trying to gauge his speed. Billy was making some circus shots, but he didn't miss when it got down to the last few balls. Before I knew it they had me stuck for $300. I pulled up, not knowing for sure how good he played. The next time I saw *Billy Johnson* was in Vegas at the Stardust, and he was beating everyone!

BRANCHING OUT

I was already the best player in Bakersfield, but I wanted to be known as the best player in the entire San Joaquin Valley. And that encompassed Fresno, which was a larger city than Bakersfield with quite a few good players. I kept hearing about "Little George", a young gun who was beating everyone up there. I sent feelers for him to come down and play me but got no response. So one day I took my wife on a short road trip to Fresno. I told her we were going on vacation, but my plan was to find George and beat him.

We made the two hour drive late in the afternoon, and I went directly to Blackstone Billiards when we got into town. This poolroom was a notorious place full of hustlers and assorted outlaws. It felt just like home to me, since I had been hanging out in places like this for the last ten years. Once inside, we were greeted by Jim Walker, the owner. Jim and me had become friendly, due to the fact we owned the two largest rooms in the Valley. He had visited my room before, and I told him I was going to pay him a visit soon. And soon was now!

I asked Jim if he would let George know I was in town, and he said that would be no problem since George comes in every night. In the meantime I could play some with "Courteous Curt", another young hustler who was already there and anxious for a game. Curt was a good looking young man, who was powerfully built and had a booming break. I played him some $10 9-Ball for an hour or two and won about ten games. I was in dead stroke and very comfortable on the Gold Crowns. I was used to playing on a tighter table in my room.

My game with Curt came to an end when George walked in. He walked right over to our table, and began to eye me up and down. I'm sure he had heard about me, and now he was sizing me up. I doubt that George was over twenty years old, but he already had that *pool hustler* look about him. Sagging jeans, a nondescript T-shirt, gunfighter eyes, pale complexion and long dirty blonde hair. My kind of guy! He had that street jargon down to a tee also. "I heard you're looking for me man." "Are you George?" I asked him. "Yeah," he said, "Whaddya got in mind?" I told him I'd like to play him some 9-Ball for whatever stakes he wanted.

Now his eyes got big. "Whatever stakes?" he asked. "Yes," I replied. I was holding close to a grand on me and was ready to play for whatever bet he chose. "How about six ahead for $300?" he inquired. "That's fine with me,"

I told him. Just like that I had my game, to see if I was really the King of the Valley. It seemed like the whole poolroom crowded around our table to sweat the match. I loved it! I always played good in front of a crowd. But so did George and we went back and forth for maybe two or three hours, no one getting more than a couple of games ahead.

George was a straight shooting son of a gun, firing balls in from everywhere. But this was the era of *push out* 9-Ball, and I outsmarted him in quite a few games. I would push out for a bank, and he would pass it back to me. I knew I could shoot the bank with impunity. If it went in I could run out, and if it missed I wouldn't leave him anything. I was winning the push out battles, but he was getting out most of the time when he had an open table. The first set must have taken five or six hours to finish, but I was a man on a mission; not just to win the money, but to prove that I was the best player in the San Joaquin Valley. For whatever reason that was all that mattered to me at that stage in my life.

I finally wore George down. I could feel him getting weak, starting to miss balls. Once I got the score to three I knew I had him. I won the first set and George was rattled. He ran around the poolroom borrowing money from whoever he could. After a few minutes he came back and told me he had $200 to play another set. At first I refused, saying our bet was $300. But finally I relented and we played five ahead for the $200. This set didn't take nearly as long, and now George was done, defeated in his own room. I felt great! Mission accomplished!

Julie and me and some *sweaters* sat down to have a beer and celebrate. I had made some new friends and they wanted to hang out with us. Cool with me and Julie loved her beer. Just when I was feeling so good, Jim Walker came over and whispered in my ear. He said, "See those guys over there against the wall." "Yeah," I said. "They are planning to rob you when you leave." I felt a sinking feeling in my stomach. I asked Jim if he could call the cops, and he told me they wouldn't come out here on a hunch. Only after something happened would they appear. I was on my own, a hundred miles from home, and the place was closing in less than an hour. I knew I should have packed my gun in the car. I could sure use it now.

I sat there and stared across the room at the three thugs. The big guy in the middle was obviously the leader. The more I looked at him the madder I got. I had driven all the way to Fresno to take on George and had played my heart out to win. Now these bums were going to take all my hard earned cash. NOTHING DOING, I decided. With that, I got up and walked directly across the room, right toward the three of them. They saw me coming, and the two guys on the side moved slightly away. I got right in the big guy's face and looked up at him, "I understand you're planning on robbing me." I was staring him dead in the eye.

Then a weird thing happened which I'll never forget or completely understand. Suddenly this big guy seemed about two feet tall, and scared out of his wits. He tried to talk but no words would come out. "Uh, uh, aahh, no, no, un uh," was about all I could understand. He was literally so frightened that he couldn't speak. I felt like I could knock him over with my little finger. My *attacker* was scared to death! Perhaps he thought I had a gun and was about to kill him. I don't really know what was going through his mind, but I was prepared to fight for my life right then. And he knew it. He could see the fire in my eyes.

The end of this story is that the bad guy ended up buying Julie and I our next beer. He wanted to be my friend.

"Toupee Jay" can still play a little.

CUE BALL DAYS

So I spent a good part of the 70's in Bakersfield running the Cue Ball, making babies and playing lots of pool. In case you didn't know, Bakersfield is a very interesting California city. For me it was like being back in Oklahoma again, with all the Okies, Arkies, Texans and other Southerners who lived there. A world apart from Los Angeles, only a hundred miles to the South. It always amazed me when I would meet someone in Bakersfield who had never been to Los Angeles, only a short drive away. It's a cloistered little "country style" community full of rednecks and hillbillies.

These countrified "rednecks" were blessed with all the associated prejudices. And this was something I had to consider while running my business. I was careful to separate whites from blacks and Hispanics as well. I would do my best to see that they were not on adjoining tables. Let them each have their own *space*.

In the beginning the biggest problem I had to face was fighting in the poolroom. These kids would fight at the drop of a hat. They were natural born scrappers and I had to put a stop to it. After a fight people automatically leave a poolroom, many times without paying their bill. Most fights occur over a girl or money. That's about it, those two reasons.

I found myself getting between combatants quite often to break up a fight. In those days I wasn't afraid to mix it up myself, and would sometimes tell a guy that if he wanted to fight he could pick on me. That statement would come back to haunt me later. For the most part the kids respected me and knew I was the owner. When I stepped in they would usually cease fighting. I didn't want to hear their explanations about who or what caused the fight. My unwritten rule was NO FIGHTING in the Cue Ball! If you want to fight, go outside in the alley and have at it. I don't care what you do out there. Just don't do it in my poolroom.

Typically, after I broke up a fight, I would ban both participants for a period of time. This was absolutely the worst punishment I could give them. The Cue Ball was their hangout, and all their friends were there. Following a banishment, I would often get apologetic phone calls and notes sent to me asking to be reinstated. I'd usually let them cool their heels for a week or so, and then let them back in. This policy worked well and within a few months fighting became a rare occurrence at The Cue Ball.

Unfortunately there were a few notable exceptions. One day a young Indian kid came sauntering in, and decided to make my poolroom his new headquarters. He was only about 5'10" tall, but must have weighed over 200 pounds. He was thickly built and solid looking. I suspect he spent his youth doing hard physical labor. This kid was a loner and had no use for anyone else, including me. He would get a set of balls and go play on a back table. If anyone came near him he would growl at them to get lost. Anti-social does not even begin to explain his behavior.

Early one day my janitor Randy was cleaning up the men's restroom, and the Indian kid decided he needed to take a pee. Randy told him he had to wait outside until he finished cleaning. That's all it took, the Indian walloped Randy and gave him a bloody nose. Randy came running out of the restroom crying, with blood spilling all over his face. He ran up to me in tears and told me what had just happened. I then went back there to deal with the situation.

As I was approaching the restroom the Indian kid came out. I asked him why he hit Randy, and he told me he had to take a pee, but Randy wouldn't let him in the restroom. I told him that was no reason to hit him, and uttered my famous line, "If you want to fight in here you can start with me". BOOM! I was on the deck! He sucker punched me so hard all I saw were stars. The fight was over before it started. I was on the floor and had no fight left in me. The kid walked out, satisfied he had shown me who's boss.

I had a huge black eye, and all the kids were talking about the beating I had taken from the big Indian kid. He must have been proud of the notoriety, because a day or two later he came back in, sat down at the counter and ordered a coke. Just another day at the 'office' for him. I wasn't there, but the girl behind the counter called me right away. I only lived five minutes away, so I headed right on down, with my .25 in my back pocket. When I got there I saw the kid, and sitting next to him was Glen Brown, the toughest kid in town. Glen had a square jaw, broad back and huge forearms. No one messed with Glen! I wasn't sure what's up, but I knew Glen liked and respected me.

My girl told me that Glen walked in and sat down, just moments before I arrived. And just that quickly, there was a heated exchange between the kid and Glen. Next thing I know they are going at it. And I mean really fighting, UFC style. There was no way I was going to break this one up. It was a *death match*, the fiercest battle I had ever seen. To this day I have never seen two men fight so long and so hard. They fought from the front of the poolroom to the back, rolling on the floor and trading punches all the way. This was a scary fight!

This went on for what seemed like an eternity, but was probably about five minutes. Finally Glen got the kid down on the ground at the back of the poolroom, where the arcade was. Back there the floor was not carpeted, just linoleum tile over cement. He had the kids head in his meaty hands and was banging it on the floor. Bang! Bang! Bang! His head was making a loud clunk every time it hit the ground. Still he wouldn't give up. Glen must have banged his head twenty times before the kid was finally unconscious. I thought he was dead. They were both covered in blood.

Glen slowly rose to his feet and walked towards me. He was a mess, his clothes torn, his face all swollen and bruised. He looked at me with a crooked grin and said, "I guess I taught him." I didn't know whether to congratulate him or tell him to get lost fast. I truly thought he had killed the kid, who was lying in a puddle of blood and not moving. No one made a move to help him either. We all just stared at him and kept our distance. I guess none of us really cared whether he lived or died. Sad but true.

Everyone was just sitting there, stunned by the fight we had just witnessed. I'm sure none of us had ever seen anything quite like it before. Like I said, it looked like a battle to the death, and maybe it was. I hadn't yet decided what to do with the body on my poolroom floor, but was contemplating calling the police, when the kid stirred. He made a small moan and began to come to. He was alive, barely. I sat there and watched as he slowly regained consciousness. I didn't offer him any help of any kind.

After maybe ten to fifteen minutes he got back on his feet and stumbled out the door. This was one hard headed kid. I figured I would never see him again. Surprise! A few weeks later he comes walking back in and sits at the counter. His face still looked swollen and he somehow seemed meek, like he didn't have any fight left in him. Maybe Glen Brown really did teach him a lesson. I went over to see what he wanted. He looked up at me sheepishly and said, "Does that guy still come in here?" "Sure," I responded, "All the time." With that the kid got up and left, never to return. I had lied to him. Glen hadn't been back in since the big fight. Last I heard Glen Brown became a preacher in Bakersfield. Thanks buddy for cleaning up my poolroom all those years ago.

One more experience sticks in my mind from those days. I had a beautiful young girl working for me named Sheila Barnes. She looked like a young

Marilyn Monroe with a beaming smile, curvaceous figure and perfect features. You know, she had it all and I was lucky to have her working for me. The guys would flock to the Cue Ball when Sheila was on duty. And she had the personality to match, outgoing and pleasant, a cheerful word for everyone and a great sense of humor to boot. Sheila was as wholesome and good looking as any woman I had ever seen.

One afternoon I walked into the Cue Ball and Sheila was on the phone, and I could see she was very upset about something. She had tears in her eyes and she was trying to hide it from me. I thought perhaps there had been a tragedy in her life, and my first instinct was to try to help her. She quickly hung up the phone and tried to act like everything was all right. I knew better. Something was really bothering her, and I wanted to find out what it was. As gently as I could I pestered her to tell me what was going on. She finally realized I was not going to relent until she told me.

She began to tell me about this guy who had been stalking her, calling her every day when she was at the poolroom. She had to answer the phone because it was a business line, and he would call her over and over again. He was saying suggestive things to her, profanities and sexual stuff that was making her very upset. She had tried to reason with him she told me, even offering to meet him if he would just come in. Of course he wouldn't do that. He preferred to harass her from a distance. Now I got the picture and I was determined to catch this guy. I thought about it the rest of the day until I came up with a plan. I had an idea how we might nail him and scare the living shit out of him. I used to call it, "giving someone the cure."

I told Sheila that she had to gain his confidence, and convince him that she wanted to meet him. The Cue Ball had floor to ceiling glass windows in front, so you could see inside from the street. Even someone in a car across the street could see who was working behind the counter, like Sheila for instance. I explained to Sheila that I wanted her to lure him into parking across the street, and wait for you to come out and walk across the street to his car. From there he could see her the whole time, and watch her walk out by herself. What he wouldn't know was I would be laying in wait for him.

Across the street from the Cue Ball was a bank with a parking lot. They chained the entrance to the parking lot at night, so you couldn't park in there. The chains were attached to a low wall that ran the length of the lot, maybe three feet high. I was going to hide behind that wall. I knew that when he parked across the street his attention would be on the Cue Ball, and Sheila behind the counter. He wouldn't be looking in the direction of the parking lot. At least I didn't think so.

It took Sheila two or three calls to convince him that she was sincere about meeting him. She told him that he didn't have to come in the Cue Ball. She would come to him! She had to convince him that she was a little intrigued by this guy who kept calling her. Finally he went for it. It was arranged that the next night when she was working, he would drive up and park across the street, right before closing time. He told her what kind of car he was driving, so she would know it was him. He also told her that if she left the Cue Ball with anyone else he would drive away.

Evening came and about twenty minutes before Sheila got off work, I left and walked the long way around the block, hid behind the wall and waited. I didn't know if the dude would actually come, and I had no idea how big he was. I didn't care, I wanted his ass. He had terrorized one of the sweetest girls I had ever met. About five minutes before her shift ended, the car he described pulled up and parked. I peeked over the wall, and could see him staring across the street at the Cue Ball and Sheila. He had his window down, so he could see better.

I quietly snuck along the wall to the driveway. Then I crouched down real low and snuck right up to his car. I stayed very low, and stealthily went around to the driver's side of the car. I was right under his open window. I jumped up suddenly, and grabbed him by the shirt on his chest. HARD! I think that moment scared ten years off his life. I yelled, "GOT YOU MOTHER FUCKER!" He was frozen in place, probably wetting his pants. What amazed me was what a clean cut looking guy he was. He was young and not so bad looking. What possessed him to make all those nasty phone calls I had no idea, but at that moment I really didn't care. I wanted to scare the living shit out of him. And I did!

He was shaking and trembling, I could feel the fear gripping him. I told him I was going to turn him over to the police. He begged me not to, telling me he would never call Sheila again. I let him suffer for a few minutes, and warned him that if I let him go, he better never call the Cue Ball again. I told him I knew what he looked like, and had his license plate number (I didn't). He was pleading with me to let him go, begging for another chance. Finally I told him, "Get the fuck out of here and don't ever come back!" He was bawling like a baby, and said meekly, "thank you, thank you." We never heard from this creepy guy again, but I often wonder if he really wised up or just tried again somewhere else. You know he actually looked a lot like Ted Bundy the serial killer. I doubt it but who knows.

TWO MORE BRAWLS

Like I said before I didn't allow sleeping in the Cue Ball. It was a poolroom not a motel. Well one day, early in the afternoon, the day girl called me at home to inform me that a guy was sound asleep in our eating area. I told her to wake him up and ask him to leave. She told me that she tried to wake him up with no luck. He was passed out cold. This irritated me so I hopped in my car and headed over there.

Sure enough, when I got there I saw a young guy out cold with his head laying on a table. I shook him and he didn't budge. I shook him harder, still no reaction other than a moan or two. I was determined to wake this asshole up, so I grabbed his long head of hair and yanked him to his feet. That worked! He was fully awake now and in a fighting mood. He was PISSED! I told him he couldn't sleep in here, and to get the Hell out! He asked me if I was going to call the police on him. I told him no, I was going to throw him out myself. He didn't want to go peacefully though.

So I grabbed him and began working him toward the front doors. He was resisting me the best he could. He was bigger than me, but I was stronger than him. I finally got him to the doorway, and he got himself wedged in, where it was hard for me to move him. All of a sudden he pulled a knife out of his boot. It was a big buck knife, and he had murderous intent in his eyes. Now he had me trapped in the doorway, waving the knife at me.

A funny thing happens when you are in a life threatening situation. Your mind slows everything down. I was anticipating each movement of his knife hand, and was dodging adeptly. He'd lunge the knife at my belly, and I'd suck back just enough to avoid it. He'd go for my throat, and I'd pull back my head. This went on for several seconds, until I could extricate myself from the trap I was in. By the way the whole time this was going on, the only words out of his mouth were, "I'm gonna kill you." He said it repeatedly. And you know what, I believed him.

Finally I was able to get away and run to the back of the poolroom. He was chasing me all the way. I got behind a pool table with balls on it, and he was running around trying to get to me. I picked up a ball and fired it at him. I threw it as hard as I could. Whoosh, it went by his head. The second ball I threw hit him square on the shoulder, and stunned him just enough for me to get around him, and escape out the front door.

I ran to my car where I had my gun. I was going to kill this bastard! I was in survival mode, and your instincts take over completely. I had a snub nose Smith and Wesson .38, loaded with hollow points. My only plan was to empty my gun in him until he wasn't moving. I ran around the corner looking for him. What I saw were three cop cars, and a bunch of cops surrounding my tormenter. He was already cuffed. My girl had called the cops the moment she saw the knife, and they must have got there in minutes.

I put the gun in the back pocket of my jeans and walked over to them. I was still pissed as Hell. I told the cops what had transpired inside, looking at the guy all the time. I asked them to let him go because I wanted to kick his ass, right there on the sidewalk. I told him that if he had kicked my butt I wouldn't have said a word. But he didn't have to pull a knife on me. After all he was bigger than me and younger too. He didn't say a word to me, just stared back in my face. The cops took him away.

Now here's the real kicker to this story. Turns out the guys name was Michael Montoya (funny how you never forget the name of someone who tried to kill you), and he had escaped from CRC (Corona Rehabilitation Center) the day before. This is a prison for men under age twenty five. He had returned to his home in Bakersfield and got high on heroin, his drug of choice. He had OD'd (overdosed) in my poolroom after shooting up all night. You want to know what he was incarcerated for? MANSLAUGHTER! He had killed someone with a knife!

You'll like this last one. But I sure didn't. Seems there was a notorious family in Bakersfield known as the "Brimage" family. They were all killers and thieves. The oldest boy Bobby, got sent to San Quentin for killing a bartender that refused to serve him just before closing time. He went out to his car and got a shotgun, and blew the guy away. Another son Danny, killed a cab driver outside Vegas after visiting a brothel. He took his money and his cab and drove back into town.

Now the youngest son was named Benny. He was a good looking kid, about eighteen years old and he loved to shoot pool. He was a good kid, so I let him clean up for me in the morning, in exchange for free pool. One day I had to pick him up at his house in Oildale. Benny wasn't quite ready, and while I was waiting in the living room Danny came out to join me. In his hand was a .357 pistol that he was very proud of. He started telling me how much disdain he had for rich folks; you know the kind who own businesses. Like me!

He was alternately pointing the loaded gun at me and laughing. It was 11 AM and I was scared shitless. But I couldn't show it. Danny tells me that he could kill me right now with one shot. Benny overheard this remark and told Danny to quit fooling around. Finally Benny comes out of the bathroom and we hustle out of there. I knew then that Danny Brimage was a very dangerous man.

A few weeks later Danny Brimage and a friend came into the Cue Ball to play pool. I put them on a table in the far back of the room, as far away from everyone that I could. Later that evening a couple of very large black men came in to play pool. They were linemen for Bakersfield College, a junior college powerhouse that recruited all over the nation. I put them in the area up front, near the far wall. I knew the Brimage boys were extremely prejudiced, so why take a chance.

No such luck. One of the black guys was heading back to the restroom and he accidently bumped Danny's cue. They had a few words and the guy proceeded on to the restroom. Danny grabbed one of the large glass mugs that we served soft drinks in, and waited.

When the guy came out of the restroom Danny let him have it full blast on the side of his head. BLAM! I could hear the crash up front. He had broken the heavy mug right across the guy's head. The big guy was now on the ground bleeding badly, with shattered glass all around him. His buddy came racing back to help, and Danny Brimage and his friend beat a hasty exit out a side door.

I ran back there to help out. We got a wet towel and gave it to his buddy to hold against his head. I told him to take him to the hospital and I would pay the bill. He got the wounded man to his feet and they left, trailing blood all the way. I thought that was the end of it. NOT!

About forty five minutes later an entourage of vehicles, full of black guys, pulled up in front of the poolroom. They got out of the cars with weapons in their hands; crowbars, baseball bats, pipes, I even saw a rifle or two. They massed up outside, with the biggest guy in front. He was obviously their leader. Then this mob poured into the Cue Ball with blood in their eyes. The uninjured lineman was right at the point, scouting around for Danny Brimage. I could hear their loud talk, "Let's tear this place apart," "Let's kick some ass," "Rip up these pool tables." This was a murderous group who were out to do some serious damage.

They wanted to destroy my poolroom, that I had worked so hard to make a success. There was no one to help me now, I was on my own. All the people in the place were cowering in fear. On instinct alone I walked from behind the counter to confront them. I walked up to the big guy in front, "Hey, I'm sorry about what happened to your friend. The guys who did it split right away. I'm willing to pay for any medical bills. Ask him?" I nodded at the guy right next to him.

The big guy looked down at me and said, "Get out of the way!" I told him, "No way, you'll have to go over me. It's my poolroom and I'm not gonna let you tear it apart." That surprised him, but his buddies were still pleading with him to let them turn over the tables and destroy everything. At least I had his attention so I said to him, "Look, it's not my fault that it happened. I'm as mad as you are. I'll never let those guys back in here. I promise you that." The big guy looked down at me and I looked right back up at him, our eyes locked. He could have easily knocked me out of the way. But he didn't.

He turned back to the mob and said, "Let's get out of here!" There was some grumbling and disagreement, but they slowly turned around and left. I never heard another word about it, and Danny Brimage never came back to the Cue Ball. It was only months later that he killed the cabby in Nevada. They caught him within a day or two and he got "Life Without Parole". Far as I know he still resides in the state pen in Nevada. That was over thirty years ago.

My rein at the Cue Ball came to an end in the late 70's. My errant lifestyle had created a wedge in our marriage, and Julie and I got a divorce. She got the house and I kept the business. It wasn't long after when a wealthy Chinese family came to me, and inquired about buying my business. I was ready for a break and took their best offer of $75,000. On the day we signed the deal, the head man brought a briefcase into my office stuffed with hundreds. He paid me in cash, my kind of guy!

Ronnie "Fast Eddie" Allen, Jack "Jersey Red" Breit, "Champagne" Ed Kelly
Three of the all time greats.

Wade Crane aka "Billy Johnson"

Buddy Hall and Louie Roberts talking things over.

"Little David" Howard "The Giant Killer"

Platis and Puckett, who's hustling who?

My brother Bruce, taken at Phoenix International Raceway.

Jose Parica "The Little Giant", he beat them all for the cash.

Jimmy Rempe, dialed in again.

A forlorn looking Louie Roberts waits his turn.

Friendly competitors, Earl and Cornbread about to mix it up.

Jay Swanson "The Gentle Giant"

"The Little Colonel" Nick Varner

Efren looks on while Nick racks.

1996 Hollywood Park Million Dollar Challenge

Top Row (left to right) Oliver Ortmann, Larry Bohn, Jose Parica, Victor Castro, Nick Mannino, Jay Helfert, Tang Hoa, Max Eberle, Mika Immonen, George Breedlove, Dennis Coulter, Tony Annigoni.

Second Row (left to right) Mike Defino, Rafael Martinez, Stevie Moore, unknown, Shannon Daulton, CJ Wiley, Paul Potier, Bob Hunter, Lou Butera.

Third Row (left to right) Takeshi Okumura, Earl Strickland, Dave Matlock, Bill Meacham, George San Souci, Joe Pacchanelli, James Boch, Ray Galaviz, Grady Mathews.

Bottom Row (left to right) Dick Weaver, Mark Jarvis, Bobby LeBlanc, Ken Taylor, Dave Chartier, Bobby Hernandez, Aaron Aragon, Richie Ambrose.

Willie Munson (on right), many times Wisconsin State Champion.

Denny Searcy, Pay Ball champion.

"Hippy Jimmy" Reid

Jim and Ewa Mataya in better days.

Jean Balukas, the man killer.

"Omaha Fats" playing his favorite game, one handed pool.

Ming and Tang, U.S. Bar Table Champions
Jay Helfert, promoter

THE LAST ROAD TRIP

I was sitting on a pile of money, a new caddy and a new girlfriend. So I did what came naturally, I went on the road. First stop Vegas and a long drawn out battle with the "Monk", aka Warren Costanzo. We played ten and twenty dollar 9-Ball for several hours, and I saw that I wasn't getting anywhere, so I quit. One of his buddies took the heat, claiming that I was quitting winners. I truly didn't know by then exactly where we stood, but we couldn't have been more than a few games apart. Anyway this guy decided to pick up the butt of Warren's cue, and threaten me with it. Thankfully, Warren stepped in and told the guy to forget about it. Lucky for him too, because my girlfriend Linda had my loaded .25 in her purse, and was quite prepared to use it. She had her hand in the purse when I looked over at her.

We headed east stopping at a few spots along the way. Nothing much happened until we reached Omaha, and hooked up with "Omaha John" Shuput. John was a top player back then, one of the best on the small tables. His wife was in the insurance business and they had a nice home. Unfortunately I had picked a bad time of year to make this trip, starting out from California in January. When we arrived in Omaha it had begun to snow. We got settled in at John's pad and he began telling me about all the good spots around Omaha. One place in particular, a bar spot, had a guy who liked to bet it up with strangers. Only thing, John couldn't go with me as that would kill our action.

John gave me a map with directions to the bar, and the keys to his little Triumph sports car. It would handle the snowy roads better than my big Eldorado. Linda didn't want to go with me; she was perfectly content to stay in the warm cozy house that night. Not me though, I was hard core. If there was a game, I was up for it. I fired up that little Triumph, and headed out looking for the bar. John's directions were perfect, and I had no trouble finding the place. It was early evening and the place was quiet, except for the pool game, and a good one at that. They were playing *challenge the table* Eight Ball for five and ten a game.

I asked if I could get in, and one guy motioned me to put my quarter up. So I did and tried to blend in, talking about the game in progress. There were three or four guys playing, and pretty soon it was my turn. It was a sociable kind of game with a little bet thrown in. Fine with me. I racked the balls and the guy asked me what I wanted to play for. I told him the last bet was okay with me, $10. I won that game and now it was my table. I held the table for several games, and the guys began to mumble about how good I was. I wasn't really holding back. That never worked well for me anyway. My strategy was just play your best and see what happens. I never lied about my game. If someone asked me how good I was, I told them I play okay. No stories about not picking up a cue for two years, or any other such nonsense. I didn't want any problems later about how I hustled them.

By now, another guy had come in and was watching me play. He was my man, the one John had described to me. He had put his quarter up and now it was his turn. I asked him what he wanted to bet and he replied, "How about $50?" John was right; this guy was ready to gamble. And so was I. $400 later he'd seen enough. Everything was cool though, there was no ill will. I beat the guy fair and square, and he just shook my hand and said that I played too good for him. It was music to my ears.

The problem was that when I walked outside there was a raging snow storm going on, and the little Triumph was covered in snow. I brushed it off enough to get in, and got it to fire up. I grew up in Ohio so I was no stranger to bad weather. I got the car out onto the snow covered street, and there was literally no traffic. It was maybe 1 AM and the streets were deserted. Conditions were bad, and I was having trouble keeping the little car going straight. Underneath the snow was a sheet of ice, that made driving that much more difficult. I was on a main drag, but had to turn onto a side street to get back to John's place. When the turn came up I was going a hair too fast, and slid off the road into a snow bank. I was stuck!

I had to walk a few blocks to find a phone to call John and tell him what happened. Luckily for me he thought it was very funny that I got myself into this predicament. He was beginning to wonder what happened to me. John got in his pick-up truck and came down and rescued me. He was glad I made a little score, and gratefully accepted the jelly roll I gave him. The next day we went back and dug the Triumph out of the snow. The weather cleared and Linda and I were off, never to see John again. He retired from pool a few years later. He was a good one though.

I purposely routed us up thru Southern Illinois so I could visit Fats at his home. He had extended an invite to me years ago, and I had his phone number with me. He lived in the little burg of Dowell, Illinois which barely registered on the map. When we got to St. Louis I gave him a call. He said, "Come on over." Fats told me that when I drive into Dowell there will be a flashing red light, and a store on the corner with a pay phone outside. He told me to stop there, and call him for further directions to his house. Sure enough his directions were good, and when I drove into Dowell I saw the light, and the store with the pay phone, just like he said.

I gave Fats a call and he answered with a big, "How ya doin?" I told him where I was and he said no problem, "Just turn right and drive out into the country. Keep following that road until you see a house with three Cadillacs in the driveway. There'll be a red one, a blue one and a gold one. THAT'S MY HOUSE!" he bellowed. I had to chuckle; I had never gotten directions like this before. Sure enough we headed out into the country a mile or so, and I see the house with a driveway full of caddies. My Eldorado fit right in beside them.

Fats welcomed us inside, and pretty soon Linda went off with his wife Evelyn into the kitchen, and Fats and I gravitated into his game room with the pool table. For the next few hours Fats held court with me, an audience of one. He propped his butt on the edge of the table, and began telling story after story about his exploits in New York, and all up and down the East Coast. He knew I was a pool player so he tailored his stories around all the good players he had fleeced.

Occasionally the girls would join us with drinks or food. It was getting to be late in the day, and I didn't want to spend the night in Dowell. But before I could excuse myself, Fats asked me, "Could you help me with something?" "Sure," I said.

He led me out to his garage. Along the wall were three large plastic buckets full of raw hamburger meat. I had no idea what they were for. He grabbed two of them, and asked me to grab the last one and follow him. I did as I was told and followed him outside onto the driveway. We stopped about halfway down the drive. Fats took the scooper out of one of his buckets, and began to dish out the hamburger meat in a line along the side of the driveway. He told me to do the same thing with my bucket. Duh, okay. I took the scooper from my bucket and began doing the same thing as Fats. I was totally clueless.

When we were all done he told me to stand with him, on the other side of the driveway. He then put two fingers in his mouth and let out one of those ear piercing whistles. Weird huh? In seconds, dogs began to appear. They came from every direction, running down the street and across fields. And I mean running! They were all flying to get there first. Where they all came from I have no idea. But within a minute or so a dozen or more dogs were happily chowing down on all that fresh meat. I had never seen an eating orgy quite like it, and Fats loved every minute of it. After each dog had his fill they would come over and thank Fats with a lick on his hand, and a kiss or two on the face. The man was in heaven. All these dogs loved him!

When the meat was all gone, Fats led me around the back of his house. He had a long row of kennels set up there, so the dogs had a place to sleep and stay out of the weather. Fats was the defacto ASPCA of Dowell. He showed me another section he had set up for cats. I think this was at his wife's request. I asked him about food for the cats. He said they don't need any, they find their own. I realized then what a humanitarian Fats was.

He was always cast as this cold blooded hustler, and the truth was he had a big heart and a soft spot for all God's creatures. I think it may have come from the upbringing he had on the streets of New York, where he had to fend for himself while still a child. He had empathy for the underdog or *under dogs* in this case.

Our trip continued east through Indiana and Ohio. I stopped in some of my old haunts along the way, and stirred up whatever action I could find. We had been on the road for almost a month, and it was late February when I set out for the big apple, New York. We were on the Pennsylvania Turnpike when the weather turned ferocious again. Within an hour it became a near blizzard. It was becoming impossible to drive. I pulled off at a rest stop and checked my map. We were not far from Scranton where Jimmy Rempe lived. I called him and told him I was on the road and only miles away. I really needed a place to get out of this storm. Jimmy said If I can make it, I should come to his place. We crawled the last few miles to Scranton, and found Jimmy's apartment building.

He was living with his girlfriend Sally (who he has been married to for thirty years now), in a very nice apartment with a fireplace. Linda and I were just happy to be out of the storm that was raging outside. Sally made us hot chocolate, and Jimmy and I kibitzed about pool players and past tourneys. Then another one of those funny things happened. Jimmy asked me if I wanted to play some pool. He knew I was on the road and had a pocketful of dough. But he was a world champion and I was a shortstop. At first I thought he was kidding me, but then I realized he was serious. He wanted to play! And I didn't want to go outside for any reason, let alone to play pool with Jim Rempe.

So I told Jimmy I couldn't play him any game; He was just too good for me. But he persisted. Finally in frustration, I said the only game I had a chance at was Banks, and he would have to spot me two balls, 8-6. Jimmy laughed

Jimmy Rempe looking elegant

and told me he never played Banks and would play me even. After some back and forth he agreed to give me a ball, 8-7. I wasn't happy that I had to leave the apartment, but somehow I felt obligated to give him action. He called ahead to the bowling alley near his home, and told them to hold the front table for him. He had a game! Me.

When we arrived at the bowling alley/poolroom, everyone was waiting for Jimmy. There must have been fifteen or twenty guys sitting around the table we were going to play on. I couldn't help but wonder what could bring all these guys out in a storm like this. I guess it was to watch Jimmy slaughter some poor schmuck. But I wasn't going peacefully. We agreed to play Full Rack Banks for $50 a game, a pretty decent bet. I figured if I lose two games I'd try to quit. I was taking a two-barrel shot at him.

The first game was close, as I had to get a feel for the table. But it was a tight Gold Crown and I liked it. I felt like I could bank well on this table. The game came down to both of us needing one ball. He missed a fairly simple cross side bank and that's all I needed, a little air. I whacked my game ball in cross side and Jimmy had to pay me in front of all his buddies. He didn't like it one bit. I didn't care anymore. All my gambling instincts were kicking in. I wanted to beat this guy, friend or not. After all, he had hustled me.

I won the next three games, none of them that close. One by one his friends melted into the woodwork, until only one or two were left. After the fourth game, Jimmy gave up. In silence we drove back to his apartment. Fortunately the storm had subsided, and I collected Linda and we bid our farewells. Jimmy and I have never talked about that game since that day, and he never asked me to play again. He's my friend and I still love him, but money's money when you're on the road.

We made it into New York late at night, and I called my Aunt Marcia in Scarsdale. Bless her heart, she told me to come over to her house. I loved staying there, it was like a Winter wonderland. They had a seven-acre estate up on a hillside with deer, rabbits and even a fox or two roaming the grounds. The house was spacious and the kitchen always stocked. We moved in! I was tired from all the driving and the gambling games. I needed a break.

After a few days I began to get restless, I had visited with all my cousins and now I wanted to hit some balls. There was a poolroom on Central Parkway, the main drag. Linda and I dropped in the next day, and I spotted two older men playing Straight Pool. Naturally, this was New York; Straight Pool is king here. I sat and watched them play. They weren't bad, good safeties, and some decent runs of over two racks. After a while I inquired where I could get a game. The friendly guys turned a little sour at my request. One of them laid his cue on the table and glared at me. "Are you a 9-Ball player?" I didn't like his tone and was not one to be intimidated. I looked him in the eye and told him "I play ALL games!" He calmed down.

Without answering me he went back to shooting. After he mopped up the rack he took a different tone with me. "There's a fellow that comes in here most nights that will play you 9-Ball. John's his name. He's pretty good though. And down the road there's a bar where they play for money. That's what you want, isn't it, a money game?" "Yes," I told him, "that's what I want." Linda and I went to dinner and came back a couple of hours later.

Now the place was busy with many tables going. Nice business I thought. I looked around until I found the 9-Ball game in progress. The tall guy holding his cue looked like a player. It was funny how I could always spot a player, even in a crowded poolroom. We meandered over.

I was right. "John" was in action, spotting some kid the seven ball for five a game. I took a seat and watched. He could play all right, but he liked to shoot at everything, not even considering playing safe. I knew I could beat him. I waited patiently until the game ended. When it was all over I piped up. "Would you like to play me some?" John looked at me kind of surprised, like who would dare talk to him like that. "What did you say?" he asked me. A little louder I said "Would you like to play me some 9-Ball?" "Are you a hustler?" he asked. I hadn't heard that line in a while. So I said, "Sure, just like you." That made him laugh, and it got him to the table. John went for a buck forty at $5 and $10 a game. I thanked him for the game and took my leave. We were headed for the bar and it was getting late.

Now this was an upscale spot, full of the well heeled drinking crowd in Scarsdale. I could smell the money. It would call for a different strategy and I knew it. I became Jay Helfert, California real estate developer on vacation. I was rich and loved to play pool. They went for it. I got invited into their friendly little game, where hundred dollar bills were flying across the table like confetti. I wanted some! My first game was for $50 with a guy who couldn't make two balls in a row. I let him shoot about five times before I won the game. I never drew the ball and shot off my thumb. Yes, shame on me, I was in full hustle mode.

I won another couple of games to guys who didn't play much better, and were more interested in getting their drinks mixed right. As soon as they took note of me winning several games, I lost! Yes, I blew a game on purpose, making the eight ball out of turn. I schmoozed and sipped my drink (UGH!), doing my best to be one of the guys. I looked and acted older than my thirty two years, and they accepted me as a rich visitor. I told them about staying with my relatives who had an estate on Fort Hill Road. Fort Hill Road was the high rent district, and I knew all about the homes in that area, even the names of some of the wealthy neighbors. When I mentioned my Uncle Bud, who was a noted Ophthalmologist in the area, one of the men knew who he was. This sealed the deal as far as they were concerned. Sorry Aunt Marcia, I had to do it!

We played until closing at 2 AM, having a great old time. All the men were hitting on Linda, who was a gorgeous little country girl with a glowing personality, and she could drink with the best of them. They kind of lost focus on me and the pool game. The games went slow, but I pulled in close to a grand that night. I knew better than to wear it out though. Those kind of games can turn sour on you in a moment. I never went back to that spot, and we headed south for warmer climes a couple of days later.

We worked our way along the Eastern seaboard, stopping in several small cities along the way. Norfolk and Richmond, Virginia; Raleigh and Fayetteville, North Carolina; Columbia, South Carolina; Augusta and Savannah, Georgia; Jacksonville, Orlando and finally we hit Miami. We had been on the road two months and I was getting tired and homesick for California. I had played a couple of dozen guys and done fairly well, booking no big losers and quite a few decent wins.

It's kind of interesting now when I go to big tournaments, back east especially. Sometimes guys will walk up to me and ask me if I remember when we played. And for the life of me I don't remember them at all. They will tell me a story about something that happened when I was in their poolroom, and I'll draw a total blank. I usually ask them how much they beat me for, and that always gets a laugh. They think I'm kidding them, because they know that's not the way the game turned out. But they like to hear it anyway. The guys I remember the best are the ones who beat me.

In Miami I hit the Congress Bowl, and ran into my old friend/enemy Pancho. Naturally he wanted to steer me all over, but I could only take Pancho in small doses. He set me up for a game with some *wealthy* older gentleman. He used the rich real estate developer line when he introduced me to him. We played Eight Ball for $20 a game. Yes, Eight Ball on a big table. That's what he liked and that's what he got. Pancho was right (as usual). The guy was very friendly, loved to chat and kept paying me off game after game. We played a couple of hours and I won about two hundred. Pancho was right there to grab his half!

Now the old Pancheroo had another game for me. He was a clean cut kid who was supposed to be from a rich family. We played some $10 9-Ball and I could see this kid had game. He kept trying to get me to raise the bet and I kept refusing. Something was funny here and I could feel it. We were staying about even but it felt like the kid was stalling. Finally I told him I'd play him five ahead for fifty. He took the bet and drowned me. It was over in about thirty minutes. I went looking for my buddy Pancho who set up the game. When I found him he feigned innocence. He acted surprised that I lost, and suggested the kid would fold for a bigger bet.

I then asked Pancho to reimburse me for $25, half of what I just lost. After all I had given him half of my winnings the day before. Nothing doing he said. He was only the *steer* man. Then why did I give him half my winnings yesterday, I asked him. Because the game was so sweet, he responded. Pancho was a dandy! I wanted to kill him, but he made everything seem so amusing you almost had to laugh. By the way the kid turned out to be none other than Mike Carella; only the second best player in Florida after Danny Diliberto. I was his *sweet* game. Thanks a lot Panch!

Finally we headed back west, and I made my rounds across the South; Mobile, New Orleans, Baton Rouge, Houston and Dallas. I played a few more guys but the one who stood out was a long haired redneck kid in Mobile. He had that real Southern drawl and a long stroke that went on forever. I played him some Eight Ball in a bar I had been steered to. The kid had to be underage but the bartender just looked the other way. I liked the kid though. He played good and was fun to play with. I couldn't help but be amused by some of his one liners, even though I couldn't seem to make any progress on the pool table. I was in dead punch, running out frequently, but so was he. Somehow I survived until the bar was closing, so I got saved by the bell. I may have lost two or three games to a very young Scotty Townsend that night. We have remained friends from that day on.

After Texas, I drove straight home non-stop. Three months on the road was more than enough for me. I was ready for new challenges.

PROMOTING AND DIRECTING (PT. 1)

During my days at the Cue Ball I tried my hand at tournaments for the first time. I played in the final Stardust tourney in 1972, and won a few matches in the One Pocket division, most notably one with Jimmy Fusco, which Eddie Robin saw fit to memorialize in his book, *Shots, Moves and Strategies.* Jimmy was the reigning Eastern States champion and I was a nobody from Bakersfield, but I hit him with some miracle shots and put him in a coma. I also played in Dayton at Joe Burn's big pool fetes in the early 70's. I had some memorable wins there as well, but one I remember best was my Bank Pool match with Willie Munson.

Willie was the Wisconsin State Champion at the time and a highly regarded player. I was the prodigal son returning to his roots, and a lot of my old buddies were there pulling for me. Before the match began, Willie sidled up next to me and asked if I'd like to make a friendly wager. He didn't know me from Adam. Little did he know I grew up in the Dayton area, and learned to play Banks from Joe Burns himself; Who just happened to be the best banker around. We agreed to play for $50. After I ran a five and a six on him, Willie gained some newfound respect for me. I beat him rather badly in the match but the best part was afterward. He reached out to shake my hand and slipped me a $50 bill. Then he said, "I had no idea you played so well." That compliment meant more to me than the money.

I also played at the ill fated Burlington, Iowa tournament in 1976, where the promoter tried to run out on the players without paying them. I was one of the people who got wind of it, and we called the cops who rounded the guy up, and made him cough up some dough. Jim Rempe won that one (for 10K) over Richie Ambrose in the finals. Sad to say but promoters like this still exist in the pool world today.

About the same time I was finishing up at the Cue Ball, Ronnie Allen was promoting his first big tourney, The World Open Eight Ball & Nine Ball Championships in Bend, Oregon. He enlisted my support and soon I was in a car with Ronnie heading for Bend. The tournament was being held at the Inn Of The Seventh Mountain, a beautiful ski resort at the foot of Mt. Bachelor. What a setting! And just about every living pool player turned out for it.

I worked with Ronnie for a couple of weeks selling Ads in the souvenir program, and also became the editor of that publication. During the actual tournament I served as Ronnie's assistant director, keeping the boards updated and refereeing matches. I had ref'd for Freddie Whalen when he put on his World Straight Pool Championships in Los Angeles, so this wasn't my maiden voyage. In the finals it came down to Mike Sigel vs. Dan Louie, and someone had to win both sets (Eight Ball and Nine Ball) to get the victory.

The local radio station decided to broadcast the finals, and they tapped me to do the commentary. Yes, I really did commentary for a pool match on the radio. And what a match it was! The two finalists kept splitting sets, and it went three rounds before Dan Louie emerged on top. This is one match I wish had been recorded on video. It was that good, and it lasted nearly five hours! Where was Pat Fleming when we needed him?

My next call to work a pool tournament came from my old buddy Richie Florence. Richie could promote as well as he could play, and had Caesars Tahoe, Budweiser and ESPN all lined up for his big 9-Ball extravaganza. It was called the Caesars Tahoe Billiard Classic, and there had never been anything like this before. Big money, big entry fees and nationwide television. The entry fee was $1,500 but every player got back $500 when he arrived. That way they would have money in their pockets at the casino. There was $30,000 in added monies, an unheard of sum back then. The total purse was over $125,000, and Mike Sigel won $30,000 for first place. Ronnie Allen got $15,000 for second. Big money in 1982!

Promoter Richie Florence with Conrad Burkman

The first year at Tahoe I was a referee, but in 1983 I became Richie's tournament director. The tourney only got bigger with more players and more money. Once again I put together a souvenir program which was a slick looking publication.

This was the year the young wunderkind Earl Strickland beat the mighty Steve Mizerak in the finals. During the final match he made a jump shot, which had to be a first on national television. Earl won $33,000 plus a new car! These successful events allowed Richie to branch out to other Caesar properties; putting on tournaments at Caesars Boardwalk in Atlantic City (also won by Sigel) and Caesars Palace in Las Vegas (a second win for Earl). I directed all these events along with Barry Behrman, who assisted me in Atlantic City.

Richie was on a good run, and things were looking up for professional pool. It all came crashing down at Caesars Palace in 1985. Everything looked good during the course of the event, and it came down to Dallas West, Terry Bell and Earl on the final day. Once again the matches were being televised by ESPN, and the players were required to sign television releases prior to the taping. This is where things got sticky. They refused to sign the releases on the grounds that they were not being paid residuals for reruns of the shows. At that time it was ESPN's custom to rerun shows multiple times. In fact they still do it today.

Signing television releases is normally a formality, and the players were getting some very bad advice. The rumor was that Bill Cayton of "Big Fights" wanted to break Richie's grip on men's pro pool, and this was a way for him to do that. Cayton was the promoter of the Legends Of Pool (also on ESPN), featuring all the old time greats. If he got Richie out of the way he could get the current champions under contract as well. ESPN went ahead and taped the matches in the hopes that the players would relent and sign the necessary releases. They never did and the shows never aired. That was the end of RDF Productions, Richie's pool promotion company. He never staged another tournament and pool lost its best promoter.

The players had essentially shot themselves in the foot. It wasn't going to be the last time either. At nearly every juncture in professional pool the players have made decisions which have proved costly to their bottom line. I attribute it to bad advice and some piss poor decision-making by the top players. Someone should have told them that repeated airings of televised matches was the surest way to stardom for any pool player. Look what it's done for Allison Fisher and the other stars of the WPBA.

I did continue directing tournaments, working at some of the most prestigious events during the 1980's and 90's. I worked with Pat Fleming and Joe Kerr on a few of the World Championships, plus just about all major events held in the western USA. I was the ref when David Howard miscued on the game ball for the title at the Disneyland Open in 1986. It gave Danny Medina the title and $12,000! I became the tournament director at the early Sands Regency events in Reno after Doug Klisch passed away. This was in the days when they would count out the winner's $10,000 prize in cash on the final table. That was always fun.

At the World Championships in 1987 Jean Balukas played Robin Bell in the finals. Jean had won something like fifteen tournaments in a row at that time. During the match Robin made the nine ball on the break a couple of times and it ticked Jean off. She made a comment to the tune of, "Beat me with skill, not luck." This irritated Robin and she filed a grievance after the match with the Women's Pro Tour. They levied a fine of $200 against Balukas which she refused to pay. She was barred from playing until she paid the fine, and she never played a professional event again. Kind of a forced retirement. Truth be known, Jean had been playing pool non-stop for twenty years, and she was burned out at age twenty nine. The pressure of always being expected to win had taken a toll on her.

Jean was the one woman of that era who could play head to head with the top men. She played in the early Sands tourneys when they had a men's and women's division. She always won the women's division, but wanted to challenge the men as well. We allowed her that opportunity, and more than a few men were upset that we let her play. Some felt that they should be allowed to play with the women if Jean could play with the men. I think the reality was that they were afraid of getting beat by her. Jean did not disappoint either, handing several top pros embarrassing losses. Mike Lebron, Keith McCready, Steve Mizerak, David Howard and Buddy Hall all felt her sting. She finished in the top sixteen in star studded fields. Who knows what would have happened if Jean had continued playing?

In 1987 I staged my first pro tournament in partnership with Paul Roberts, a local PR man. We put it on at the Biltmore Hotel in downtown Los Angeles, and invited sixty four players, four of them women. It was a huge success with crowds lined up out the door every day. We used a new format for a professional pool tournament. The matches were single elimination, two out of three sets, similar to a tennis tournament. The tournament was played on the toughest Peter Vitalie tables you could ever imagine, and that was mostly my fault. I had requested Gil Atkisson, the owner of Vitalie, make the tables as tough as possible. He did that and then some! Four inch pockets with deep set slate made for some interesting situations. A ball could be lodged so deeply in the pocket that you couldn't hit it going down the rail with the cue ball. The tables gave the players fits.

The tournament was not without it's controversial moments. In the semifinal match between Efren Reyes and Mike Sigel, the referee nodded out in his chair and missed a possible foul by Efren. I had to come down on the floor (I was the TD), and have both players tell me their version of what happened. All the while the crowd (with dozens of Filipinos) was screaming and yelling at the ref and me. My decision was that Efren had indeed fouled and Sigel would get *Ball In Hand*. The crowd went crazy, and Efren proceeded to pack up his cue while Sigel was running out. It looked like I would have a riot on my hands. Sigel ended up with a nine ball shot down the rail at a very small pocket opening. He hung the nine! Efren reached in his case, extracted his cue and made the nine ball. Thank God! Sigel did ultimately win the match and played Buddy Hall in the finals. The payoff was $15,000 for first and $7,000 for second. Buddy won a lackluster final, and later I found out they made a deal to split the money. Turns out this was not unusual in the world of big time pool, where there were few big paydays. All these years later and not much has changed.

The following year I promoted the Southern California Open on my own, with the sponsorship of the Southern California Billiard Dealers Association. This event featured thirty two top guns, and was won by David Howard over Efren Reyes in a stirring final match. No deal this time and David picked up 10K! Again we had packed crowds daily at the Santa Ana Elks Lodge, where it was being held. My career as a promoter was now launched in earnest.

At that time, I was also promoting regional tournaments at the brand new Orange County Sports Arena. At the Sports Arena I was doing a monthly tournament that featured a $55 entry fee and was limited to thirty two players. We always filled the field, and the house added $400 to make it a $2,000 purse. It was single elimination, and it paid $800 to the winner, second place got $400, third and fourth $200 each, and fifth thru eighth places got $100. The $5 *juice* on each entry went to me for running the tournament. I made a buck sixty on each one.

This monthly event drew all the best players in Southern California, and big crowds of spectators. Chuck Markulis had visited the Sports Arena and

Chuck Markulis

Cecil "Buddy" Hall, Chuck's favorite player

liked what he saw. He owned a small pool room called Varsity Billiards, but he wanted a bigger place where he could hold tournaments. Chuck was interested in putting on much larger events, I would soon come to find out. He called me one day and asked me to meet him in Bellflower. I drove down and met him at the site of a vacant building, that used to be a furniture store. He took me inside and it was huge, as big as the Sports Arena. He said he planned to put a poolroom in here, and have a large tournament area with seating for spectators. He then handed me a sheet of paper showing the building's dimensions, and asked me to help him lay it out. That very day Chuck and I designed the floor plan for Hard Times Billiards, which included a tournament arena with ten tables and seating for 250 spectators.

We began having tournaments at Hard Times in 1988, and they became the biggest and best poolroom events ever held anywhere. Chuck had asked me what it would take to get the top players. I told him that if we did it the week after the Sands tourney, many players would come out west for both events. We needed major added money, and not the typical one or two thousand that many rooms had been adding. I told Chuck that $10,000 added should do the trick. He looked at me sideways and said, "Let's do it!" We did just that, and sure enough we drew world class fields to Hard Times. All the big guns came out, and players like Buddy Hall, Earl Strickland, Nick Varner, David Howard and Jay Swanson emerged as champions. Chuck liked to put the winner's prize money in a nice fat envelope, and I would hand it to them. You should have seen their faces when they got that envelope with $6,000 stuffed in it. You'd think they won an Oscar or something.

In 1990 I made a proposal to George Hardie, who was the general manager of the Bicycle Club Casino, to produce a pool tournament there. George brought in Robert Turner to work with me, and together we created the Bicycle Club Invitationals. Like the Sands, these were twice yearly events with good prize money. The West Coast now had four major tournaments a year, plus a couple more good ones at Hard Times in Bellflower. Times were good for pool out west, until Don Mackey entered the scene. I'll get back to that later.

Let's take a break from running tournaments for a moment and talk about another side of the pool coin.

Keith, "I just talked to Mike."

Jay, "Yeah, what did he say?"

Keith, "When I told him I wanted to play for the whole thing, he looked like he was going to shit his pants! All the blood rushed out of him!"

Jay, "Okay so you're playing for the whole twenty five thousand, right?"

Keith, "Yeah, no deal."

Jay, "Okay go ahead and play, you'll be fine now."

Keith went back in there and bombed Mike Lebron 9-3 for all the cheese! We were $25,000 richer! Hallelujah baby! I will give props to Mike too, who was a great player. He went on to get his revenge a couple of years later at the U.S. Open, beating Keith and all the other big names, and becoming the oldest man to win this title at age fifty four.

I made some other good scores with Keith, most notably at the tourneys being held twice a year at the Sands in Reno. Keith had several top six finishes, and we were betting pretty good on a lot of his matches. The trick with Keith was keeping track of him, and making sure he showed up to play his matches. I'll never forget one year at the Sands, when he failed to show for his match when he was in the final four on the winner's side. That match was only worth an extra $2,000 if he won.

We found him shacked up somewhere, and got him back just in time to play Nick Varner on the loser's side. Keith was badly hung over and got bounced out quickly. But not before he bet a thousand on the match with Nick, which I then had to pay out of the $2,200 Keith won for 5th-6th place. To say I was pissed is a mild understatement.

We had better luck in Phoenix later that year, when they had their State Championships. It was an All Around event with three divisions; 9-Ball, Eight Ball and Seven Ball. First prize in each division was $1,500, and the overall winner got a $2,000 bonus. Keith trounced the field winning the 9-Ball and the Eight Ball, and getting second in the Seven Ball for another "G" Note. Altogether we won $6,000 on a trip that cost around $500 total.

I took $500 off the top and split the balance with Keith. Then I caught the next plane home. Keith decided to stick around and try to parlay his winnings at Kolby's, a notorious gambling mecca in Phoenix. He made a bad game with someone (maybe Eddie Brown), and ending up blowing all his cash. He then went to the owner of Kolby's and asked to borrow a thousand until I got there. He said I was good for it. He failed to mention

The evil one, Keith McCready

that I had already gone home. Somehow Keith managed to lose two thousand on my bill without me even being there. I told you he moved good!

Keith then left the premises promising to get the money from me. That was his escape plan. The next day I get a call at home from the bad ass who owned Kolby's, threatening me with bodily harm if I don't make good on Keith's losses.

This was the first I had heard about Keith's game from the night before. I tried explaining this to the guy, but he was very stubborn. Finally I was able to convince him that I wasn't even in Phoenix that night. I offered to send him a copy of my plane ticket. That's when he realized he had been had by Keith. He vowed to get Keith and make him pay.

And he did too! When we went back a few years later for the Ronnie Allen - Danny Diliberto One Pocket match, guess who was waiting for Keith. He grabbed Keith and held him by the throat against the wall. It was not looking too good for him, until Harry Platis intervened and bailed Keith out with the dough. Harry to the rescue! After that experience my stake horsing days with Keith nearly came to a halt. But there was one last adventure that Keith and I had, and it was the one that made him famous.

THE COLOR OF MONEY BECKONS

Martin Scorsese, the movie director, and Richard Price, a well known screenwriter, showed up at the ill fated Caesars Palace 9-Ball Classic in 1985. I heard they were working on a new pool movie, and being the tournament director, I did my best to accommodate them. I saw Scorsese again later that year at the U.S. Open in Norfolk, Virginia, at Barry Behrman's Q Master Billiards.

When Scorsese arrived, Barry brought him over to me, and asked me to show him around. With Scorsese was a handsome young man, who I recognized as Tom Cruise. He said hello to me and extended his hand saying only, "Hi, I'm Tom." I shook his hand, and asked him if he was the guy I saw dancing around in his underwear in *Risky Business*. He said "Yeah that was me." We hit if off pretty good, and for the rest of the day we sat in the stands watching the matches.

Tom was a very bright young man, and asked many questions about why the players did certain things. He wanted to know why they chalked their cue a certain way, why they used powder and a cloth on their cue, and why they broke the balls from different angles. I patiently answered all his questions, while Scorsese wandered around doing his own investigation of the happenings at Q Master. When Martin returned he wanted to know what was going on in the back room, behind the curtains. I told him the big money games were going on back there, and it was not open to the public.

Naturally he wanted to see what was happening behind the curtains. So I talked with Barry and got them into the back room. The only stipulation was they had to stay against the wall and be quiet. The three of us entered the back room together, where there were three or four money games underway. The biggest game pitted Keith McCready against Danny Medina. They were playing a "race to eleven" for $1,500 and Keith was in full gear, laughing and joking with all the onlookers. He was both hysterical and brilliant at the same time, and I could tell Scorsese was enthralled by him.

After the tournament we all went our separate ways, but not before Scorsese asked me how to get in contact with Keith. I explained to him that Keith had no real home, he lived on the road. But he was always in touch with me (usually needing financial assistance), and I could find him if they needed to get in touch with him. I gave Scorsese my home phone number, and sure enough a few weeks later I got a call from his office. It was the casting director, Barbara Del Fina, looking for Keith. They wanted him to come to Chicago to audition for a part in their new movie, *The Color Of Money*.

I quickly located Keith and told him the good news. He wasn't that impressed, and told me he didn't want to fly to Chicago on his dime (his words). I called Del Fina back and explained that Keith wasn't really that interested in flying to Chicago for an audition. She tried to convince me, telling me what a big deal this was, and how important Scorsese was. All this meant little to Keith. I explained to her that Keith knew nothing about the film making business, and could care less if he was in a movie. If they could take care of all his expenses, he might agree to come. He was currently tied up negotiating pool games and playing the ponies. Those were his priorities.

She relayed this information to Scorsese, and called me back the next day. They would pay Keith's air fare and put him up in a hotel, if he would come to Chicago for the audition. Keith figured he might find some good action there, so he agreed to go. Before he came, Scorsese wanted him to look at the script, and review the part they wanted him to play. The script was overnighted to me, and Keith came over to my house to read it. The character was named Grady Seasons, and he was supposed to be the best money player in the world. That part Keith liked!

We read the script and there were maybe six lines for Grady Seasons, and Keith didn't like any of them. He told me, "I would never say anything like that." So I asked him to tell me what he would say, and together in my den we rewrote the lines for Grady Seasons, and put them in the margin of the script. All this was done with the approval of Scorsese, who after hearing that Keith didn't like the lines, suggested we rewrite them. And that's exactly what we did.

A few days later Keith was off to Chicago, ticket in hand. Once he showed up, the other actors trying for the part of Grady Seasons had no chance. He walked into Scorsese's office and it belonged to him. All the new lines we had written were kept intact, and his part even got expanded. Keith ended up staying several weeks on the set, and was well paid for his work. I met him at the end of the shoot, and accompanied him to the wrap party. I could see Keith was well liked by the crew, and he and Cruise had become fast friends.

The Classic Cup tournament was scheduled to begin outside Chicago a few days later, so the timing couldn't have been better. Or at least I thought so.

Keith McCready, aka Grady Seasons with Dave Piona

On the first night of the tournament Keith blew most of his paycheck to Efren playing One Pocket, and I was in for a grand myself before I pulled up. I was also staking Danny Medina in this tourney, and he finished third, enough to get me winners for the trip. I'll tell you about my little road trip with Danny later.

A few months later they had dual Premieres for *The Color Of Money*, one in New York and one in Los Angeles. I was hired to provide a few players to entertain the crowd at the 'after' party, held at the very ritzy Chasen's restaurant. Keith, Kim Davenport and Robin Bell came with me to Chasen's, where they had two tables set up in the lobby. These were the same Murray tables that had been used in the final two scenes of the movie, and they had plaques mounted in the rail attesting to that.

A who's who of Hollywood walked through that lobby, but very few stopped to play pool with us. Keith ran off to drink and party with his buddies from the filming, leaving the rest of us to stay obediently at our posts, with the pool tables. We shot trick shots and entertained whoever stopped to visit. Only a few of the celebrities wanted to play pool, and I can only remember Lynn Swann hanging out for more than one game.

Of interest to me was the silent auction going on for these two tables. No one was bidding, and I felt they may have value as collector's items, after the movie came out. I asked if I could bid and was told yes, that all money raised from the auction was going to charity. At the end of the night one table had a high bid of $1,500, and the other table had a single $1,000 bid. I went ahead and bid $1,100 for this table, just to see what would happen. The next day I got a call from someone saying I had won the table. They asked me where I wanted it delivered too. I was renting a house in West Los Angeles, and the only room large enough was the living room. A week later, the soon to be "most famous pool table in the world" was in my living room, plaque and all.

Who knew that the movie was going to be such a success? I sure didn't. It was an even bigger hit in Japan, and it started a billiards boom in that country which has never abated. A few months after the release of the movie I got a call from Japan. Someone had tracked me down as the owner of the table used in the final scene of *The Color Of Money*. They wanted to know if I would sell the table. Of course I said no, it was not for sale. "Would you take $5,000?" I was asked. "No I wouldn't," I replied. I had another number in mind, $10,000! After a few days of negotiating I got my price, and a bank check arrived a few days later. A couple of days after that the same Murray crew who had installed the table came out and picked it up. It was being transported to Tokyo to be put on display in a club aptly named The Los Angeles Club.

A year or so after my table sale, I was hired to be a consultant on the television crew for the International 9-Ball Championship, being played in Tokyo. While I was there, the general manager of the Los Angeles Clubs (of which there were several) invited me to accompany him to visit the main club. His name was Kenzo Kanda, and he was a handsome young man, who spoke fluent English. Even though I only spent a few days with him, I will never forget this gracious gentleman.

Kenzo took me to a very upscale and private Los Angeles Club. You had to be a member just to get in. Only the wealthiest pool players in Tokyo got to play there. I was invited to spar with the house pro who was a decent player. He wanted me to show him a few things about One Pocket, because he knew this was the big gambling game in America. While we were practicing I was waited on hand and foot. Pretty young gals in kimonos brought me hot tea and snacks on ornate platters, and afterward a hot towel to wipe my hands and face with. The room we played in had six or seven Brunswick pool tables, and luxurious furniture. It was very cozy with plush couches and big soft chairs. I could get used to this, and the girls were little dolls. Oh, I said that already.

Now for the big surprise. A girl came to me holding a platter with a gold envelope on it. I had no idea what this was. But I was told to take it, it was for me. I opened the envelope and inside was a gold membership card for the Los Angeles Club. It said Jay Helfert was a Lifetime Member of the Los Angeles Club. My name had been engraved on the metal card. I was floored, shocked and amazed! I could not believe what they had done. Why me, and not Mike Sigel or Nick Varner, who were also there? This was in 1989, and regrettably I have never been back to Japan since. Such warmth and hospitality I had never experienced before in my life.

Another interesting aspect of that trip was all the side action being bet on matches. Here we had the best American players; Sigel, Varner, Rempe and Strickland up against the top Japanese guys, and people were coming out of the woodwork to bet hundreds, *even*, on the locals. I think that Japan was flush with American dollars back then, as they were pulling stacks of money out to bet with. At first I was hesitant, since I was hired to do a job here, but when I saw the American players gambling on the matches I decided to take a piece myself. I must have bet on ten matches and won them all, except for one bet I made on a Lou Butera match.

When the tournament was over, the promoter Charlie Takahashi, had us meet him in his office to settle up. Earl had won the tournament and the $40,000 first prize. Sigel was second and won $20,000. Varner and Rempe took the next two spots for ten grand each. Charlie escorted us into his private office, and proceeded to pull out several huge stacks of brand new one hundred dollar bills. Where and how he got all that money was a mystery to me. This stuff was new, fresh from the mint, all in numerical order, and we were in Tokyo. Charlie handed me $4,000 for my work, which amounted to hanging out with the players for the most part. Then he paid all the other guys with big stacks of cash. You should have seen those happy faces. Christmas came early that year!

Earl had so much money he was afraid to carry it all through customs. He gave me and a few other people $5,000 each to carry back for him. When I got home I put Earl's 5K in my bank account. I didn't see him again until the BCA Trade Show months later. I handed him a bank check for $5,135. He was shocked. First of all, he appeared to have forgotten he had given me the money, and second he couldn't believe he was getting it back, *with interest*. He must have told that story to everyone at the Trade Show that week, he was so thrilled.

STAKING SOME MORE PLAYERS

I got involved in staking several more pool players during and after my experiences with Keith. I put Bob Hunter in action a few times and he did well, even finishing second in one fairly big event back East. I think Buddy beat him in the finals. Bob was a gem, he called me after the tournament and asked if I wanted him to wire the money to me. I told him that's okay, just wait until he returns to the West Coast.

After he returned from this trip, Bob and his wife Julie had an opportunity to go in partners with Kelly Simpson in a new poolroom in Carson City, Nevada. It would be called Cuephoria. They needed $12,000 for their end of the deal, and had only half that amount. I agreed to loan them the other $6,000, and did so just on their word. A year later they sent me back my $6,000 with interest. Bob was as honorable a guy as I ever met in the pool business, and he turned out to be a damn good cue maker as well.

I also put Ronnie Allen in action a couple of times. The first time was for the Red's One Pocket tournament in Houston in January, 1985. Ronnie made it to the finals, where he had to play Jeff Carter. It was a good match, but Ronnie prevailed and we won $4,000, plus a $500 gift certificate to a local men's clothing store. We split the money and Ronnie took off for dinner. I found out later he ran down to the store and quickly bought $500 worth of clothes for himself. I didn't even get a t-shirt. Oh well, at least I got my two grand before he hit the track.

Another one of my prize horses was Louie Roberts, the most charismatic pool player I have ever known. He attracted crowds to watch him play everywhere he went, and the girls went gaga over him. But he was also very self-destructive, with inner demons he could not control.

Our first trip was to Austin, for Sid Mann's $30,000 Villa Capri Open, in 1984. Louie only did fair in the tourney, finishing tied for 7th I believe. We got back maybe $750, enough to cover expenses only. But one night during the event we headed out to Moyers, where all the action was. Louie loved to play for the cash, and he proceeded to blitz the whole pool room, giving up weight to everyone and bombing them one after another. We won several thousand dollars that night, and I was finally able to drag him out of there around 6 AM. We needed to get going, because Louie had a match at 2 PM that same day.

On the way out of the parking lot a big caddy pulls in, with Jimmy King a

109

"St. Louie Louie" Roberts

"Denver Danny" Medina

notorious hustler driving. He sees Louie in my car, and waves a stack of cash out the window and yells to Louie, "Where you going? Let's play some." I told Louie we had to go because he had a big match later that day. Louie insisted I stop and let him out, promising me he would be back in time to play. He wanted me to give him all the money we had just won. That I would not do, but I did give him half of it, something like $1,600. I went back to the motel and fell sound asleep. I woke up about Noon, to the sound of Louie creeping in the door. He was broke of course, and played his next match on zero sleep and lost badly. Louie did manage to win one or two more matches on the loser's side, before being put out. If he had come back with me that morning, he might have won that tournament, and the $10,000 first prize.

It was a couple of years later when I decided to give Louie one more chance. We agreed to meet in Chicago for the 1987 Classic Cup. I would once again be staking him and paying all the expenses. The tournament was being held at the beautiful Pheasant Run Resort outside Chicago. The hotel had a large man made lake that came right up to the railing on our private patio. Louie had brought his girlfriend along with him, and the three of us shared the room. He was doing okay in the tourney until he started drinking. That was always Louie's downfall. He lost a match to Ron Casanzio, a player he should have beaten easily, and went straight to the bar and got roaring drunk.

Louie disappeared for hours, and no one knew where he went. Late that night he showed up back at our room, totally plastered. He got into an argument with his girlfriend, and jumped off the railing into the water. Louie was swimming around in the lake, and I was afraid he would drown. I finally convinced him to get out of the water, before he got himself arrested. He climbed back over the railing sopping wet. He took off all his clothes except his under shorts, and once again began arguing with his girl. Then he decided to run out into the hall dressed only in his undies. I had to run him down, and drag him back to the room with the assistance of a security guard. We were in danger of getting kicked out of the hotel, and I was scheduled to do commentary on the television broadcast the next day. Somehow I had to calm Louie down and get some rest myself.

No such luck! The argument ensued again, and Louie punched the poor girl in the face, knocking her to the floor. She was only trying to keep him from running outside, and getting us kicked out of the hotel. I jumped on Louie and wrestled him onto the bed. We fought for maybe ten minutes, before he gave up from exhaustion. I had him pinned down on the bed in a choke hold. I asked him if he would remain calm if I let him go. He said yes, so I released my hold on him. He jumped up off the bed and ran for the door. Here we go again, another few minutes of fighting and once more I pinned him down on the bed. He begged me to let him go, but I refused this time. I held Louie down for maybe half an hour, until he fell asleep in my arms. Then I passed out beside him. I doubt that I got more than three or four hours sleep that night.

I had a lot better luck staking Danny Medina. We went on the road in the mid 80's, traveling through Kentucky, Ohio, Indiana and Illinois. There were big tournaments being held in Lexington, Kentucky and then the Classic Cup in Chicago two weeks later. In the first event, Danny played in both Divisions, Bank Pool and 9-Ball. He finished tied for fifth in Banks for $500, and fourth in the 9-Ball for another $1,800. Not bad for starters. But the big surprise was how I did in the Banks. I lost my opening match to Earl, who just blitzed me. He beat me 5-0 in less than thirty minutes. I was totally pissed at myself, and decided to practice all night to get in stroke.

I played for eight or nine hours straight, until I felt like I could make any bank. It was about 7 AM when I quit, and my next match was at 6 PM that night. I went up and got some sleep, and came down ready to play. My match was with Mike Lebron, who was installed as a big favorite over me. The betting line was that I wouldn't win two games. I bet $200 and had Danny bet another $200 for me. I beat Mike 5-3. Cha-ching, $400! Then I had to play "Freddie The Beard" the next day, and once again I'm the big dog. This time the *book* is saying I won't three. I bet another $200 and had Danny do the same. I won again 5-3. Cha-ching, $400 more! My next match that night was with Louie Lemke. All of a sudden I became even money. Once again Danny and I got down for $400 and I won 5-4. I was $1,200 winners in two days!

Now I was in the money and had to play Dave Bollman. I wasn't as thrilled with this match as Dave was playing great right then. No bet! He had me 4-2 and I won the next two games to go hill-hill. I broke and made a ball and proceeded to run out, or almost anyway. I made four banks in a row, but didn't have a decent shot at my game ball. I could have, and should have played safe. But I was feeling it and wanted to shoot. I decided to go for a difficult long rail bank from a bad angle. I had to turn the cue ball loose to shoot this shot, but I just couldn't make myself play safe. So I fired away and made the shot! The cue ball went three rails and scratched in the corner. I still had Dave 3-0, but he came back and won the game, and put me out. I told you he was playing good!

This was the tourney where Nick Varner played Parica in the finals. They installed me as the referee for this match, racking the balls and calling hits. Remember this is in Kentucky, Varner country, and Parica is not a crowd favorite in this spot. Nicky gets off to a big lead, and up comes a shot (after the break) where he has the cue ball almost touching the one ball, and the nine ball is right in line with both of them. He slams the shot and makes the nine cross side. It's an obvious double hit on the cue ball, so I call FOUL very loud. The crowd erupts, spewing verbal venom down on me. I look at Nick, and tell him he fouled by hitting the cue ball twice on that shot. He scratches his head and says, "You know, maybe I did." The crowd calms down when they hear that. From that point on Parica mounts a comeback and beats Nicky on the hill.

After the Lexington tourney, Danny and I headed north to Ohio. No one beat Danny in Cincinnati or Dayton. No big games but still winners another thou. We got to Indianapolis, and Danny played Stevie O. on a bar table. No one could beat Stevie back then, or at least that's what I was told by the local *sweaters*. One small problem, Danny didn't know he was supposed to lose. And he didn't either. His big break wore poor Stevie out. That and the fact he didn't miss a ball for something like four hours.

Now we drove up to Chicago. Danny was in dead punch and I didn't really care who he played. We were already over five thousand winners in less than two weeks, so I had some coin to play with. We went to the Billiard Cafe where all the players were hanging out. The first guy that asks Danny to play is Freddie The Beard, and naturally he wants to play some Banks. Freddie has his well heeled backer "Big Wayne" with him, and he wants to bet $500 a game. I'm not so thrilled with the game, and it's a big bet. I pull Danny aside and ask him how he feels about playing Banks with Freddie. The ever stoic Mr. Medina looks me in the eye and says, "No problem, I'll beat him."

This was big action and I was nervous, but I knew how good Danny was playing right then, so I let him go. They were playing Full Rack Banks which can be long games, and Wayne and I sat next to each other to exchange money. Danny won the first game and Wayne handed me five "C" notes. Sweet! Now he looks at me and asks, "Do you play Banks?" Duh, what's up with this I thought? Is this guy kidding me? I said, "Sure, I play a little." Now he asks if I'd like to play some with him. My mind is racing. I'm already involved in the biggest action of our trip, and the backer wants to get down with me.

So I ask him what he has in mind. He says how about we play some friendly Banks (his words), "Short Rack" for only fifty a game. Okay, why not. I tell Danny I'm going to play some myself, and hand him two thousand to cover his action. He just gives me that little smirk of his and says go ahead. Wayne hands a stack of bills to Freddie, and off we go. He guides me to the far table at the front of the room, and we get right into it. Fifty a pop, Short Rack Banks, my kind of game. We end up playing all night, right until the place is closing, same as Danny and Freddie. Danny turned out to be the best player that night, winning five games and $2,500. Meanwhile I blitzed Wayne for fifteen games and $750 more! He may have won one game the whole time we played. He never said boo or whimpered one bit. He took it like a man.

After a one day detour to go to the "wrap" party for *The Color Of Money*, we were off to Aurora and the Classic Cup. The usual strong field was assembled, sixty four of the best players in the country. But Danny was loose as a goose and so was I. We were big winners on this trip and feeling no pain. Danny played great and had a shot to win the whole thing, but he lost a match to Dave Bollman (I told you he was playing good!) on the winner's side, and then Parica put him out in third place. Bollman ended up beating Parica for the title. Danny won $2,750 for third place, our last score of the trip. A few days later I said goodbye to Danny and he left for Colorado, but not before we chopped up nearly ten grand in winnings. And that's after all expenses were paid!

Dave Bollman

THE ROAD MAN

I'm going to back track a couple of years, because the following is one of my favorite road stories, and you'll soon see why. Chris MacDonald was known as "The Road Man" back then, because he crisscrossed the country in his camper truck for several years. He was traveling with his girlfriend Julie Jay, who also became a fixture on the 80's and 90's pool scene. Julie was a voluptuous little dish that wore hippy style garb, and loved nothing more than to smoke pot and hang out with the guys. Chris was a more than decent player, excelling at One Pocket and Banks. I put him in a few big tourneys back then and he never failed to cash, and even had a couple of top five finishes.

In 1984 we met up at the BCA Trade Show in Ft. Worth, Texas. I was there mainly because Fats was getting inducted into the Hall Of Fame, and he invited me to join him, along with U.J. Puckett, who lived in Fort Worth. Chris and Julie were there because of the amateur tournaments being held in conjunction with the trade show, and Chris wanted to plunder the natives for a dollar or two. There weren't many money games to be had though, and Chris was having trouble getting in action. He had become fairly well known, due to his success in the tournaments the last couple of years.

There was one game he could get in though. It was an open Ten Ball Ring Game on the bar table, $20 a man. It was going every night, and all the best players were jumping in. But it was high-risk; a player might not get a shot for five or six games. Chris asked me to put him in the game, and I did, giving him $200. He proceeded to eat the game up, winning nearly $800 over the course of a couple hours. While Chris was playing, a local guy informed me about a black pimp who loved to play One Pocket, and was hanging out at Rusty's in Dallas every night. He was supposed to be going off for big scores.

After the bar table game broke (mostly thanks to Chris), we headed over to Dallas in my rented Lincoln Town Car. It was Chris, Julie, myself and Lee Simon, a poolroom owner from Northern California. Rusty's was an all night joint, and in full swing when we arrived. Remarkably, the pimp we heard about had just arrived minutes before we got there, and was practicing on his favorite table. A few of the locals were talking to him about playing, but he wasn't having anything to do with them. On the sidelines watching the action I spotted Hawaiian Brian, Swanee and Jack Cooney, only three of the top hustlers in the country. I knew this had to be a good spot to attract these guys.

We waited patiently while the local hustlers tried to talk Marcus ? (I'm guessing here) into playing. When they gave up I sent Chris over to do his thing. Chris was good at his art, and within minutes he came back and said he was going to give the guy 8-7 and the break for $100 a game. I gave him $400 and grabbed a seat near the table. We were in action with the biggest sucker in the joint, or at least I thought he was. After two or three games, a very large man approached me and quietly said, "Play a little bit of that Tonk?" I had no idea who he was, and when I saw his huge hands I was sure he was a card mechanic.

I did know how to play Tonk, and had learned from some of the best in my days at Winks pool room in Dayton. We were already over a $1,000 winner for the night, so I said what the heck, let's see what he's got. I could always quit if I felt like I was getting cheated. We started out for ten and twenty a game, meaning if you go down and win you get ten dollars, and if you go all the way out you get twenty dollars. I started right out winning and quickly got $100 ahead. He then asked me to raise the bet to twenty and forty. Now that's a pretty healthy bet, and I was still not sure if I was getting hustled.

I made Norm (my new card playing friend) wait a while, until I got $200 ahead. Now I was ready to raise the bet. A funny thing happened (I know, I keep saying that), nothing changed. I went right on winning, stuffing twenty dollar bills in my pockets game after game. It wasn't long before I got him stuck over $500. Now he wanted to play for fifty and a hundred, a very serious bet. If he cheated me now I would quit him winners, so I decided to let him jack it up again. He had a huge bankroll that he kept peeling money off of.

The game continued to go my way, and he was paying me in fifty and hundred dollar bills, which I was stuffing into every pocket. Tonk is a fast game and can be over in less than a minute. A long game takes maybe five minutes. I was starting to win some big money, and Chris' pool game had come to an end, with him making another nice score. Now Chris, Julie and Lee had to wait for me. Norm was not ready to quit, so we continued our "friendly" Tonk game. His bankroll was starting to shrink, and my pockets were bulging. About this time another man joined us, a friend of Norm's. He wanted to sit behind me and sweat my action. Nothing doing I told him, you can sweat your man Norm if you like.

So this new guy watches a couple of hands, and Norm asks me if I would like to play some with his friend. I was sure this guy was the card mechanic, so I declined his offer to change players. I told him we were doing just fine, and I didn't want to make any changes. Our game continued until Norm went broke, peeling off his last few bills to pay me. I had won several thousand dollars from him, but I had no idea exactly how much. Once again his friend asked me if I would *catch* a few hands with him. I was so far ahead I figured why not. Now I had a new opponent, but he didn't play any better than Norm, and had an equally large bankroll.

About seven or eight in the morning, I had won all his money too. After the last game he didn't have enough money left to pay me. He had maybe thirty some dollars left in his pocket. I told him to forget it, it was no big deal. In fact I even offered him some *walking around* money if he needed it. Nothing doing he said, I would get paid. With that, he goes up to the bar and talks to the girl behind the counter. A minute later he comes back with a stack of one dollar bills, bundled together in packs of twenty. This had to be the change for the bar, and the girl had given it to him so he could pay me for the last game. I refused at first but he insisted I take it. Actually I had no place to put it, my pockets were that full.

Now that the Tonk game was over, my next thought was how do we get out of here safely with all that money. A lot of people had observed the game, and I was afraid someone might be laying in wait for me. I told Julie to go outside and look around, just to make sure the coast was clear. She came back in a minute, and said no one was out there and the parking lot was almost empty. We hastily made our exit, and jumped in the car and blew out of there. I was feeling ecstatic! I had made a monster score and gotten out with the money. We drove back to Fort Worth and dropped off Lee at his hotel, and then we went over to Chris and Julie's camper. Inside, I piled all the money on their little table, and asked Julie to help me count it. The bills were all crumpled up and wrinkled. I like my bills neatly folded, but I had no time for that at Rusty's.

First things first, and Chris hands me $1,200. He had won another $800 in the One Pocket game. I chopped that with him, four hundred apiece. Now for the juicy score. It took Julie and I several minutes to straighten out all the money, sort it and count it. I had won over $7,000! Sweetness! It put a nice big bulge in my jeans. Plus I was $800 winner from the money Chris made that night. It was my biggest score to date. I tried to give Chris and Julie some money, but Chris refused saying that it was my money, I had won it on my own. I swear to God he wouldn't take a dime no matter how hard I tried.

Chris MacDonald, "The Road Man"

How many pool players are there on the planet like Chris MacDonald? I'm guessing one! Not having any luck with him, I got out of the camper and Julie walked me to my car. Before I got in I slipped her the pile of ones ($100) and told her to buy herself something. Julie was a little more pragmatic than Chris. She accepted it!

An epilogue to the above story, is that all the aforementioned hustlers who were at Rusty's that night never said boo to me. They didn't want to blow my cover by acknowledging that they knew me. Now that's a true hustler, who knows when to shut up and play dumb.

Months later when I ran into Jack, he told me that Norm and his partner own the two biggest bingo parlors in Dallas, and he also likes to play One Pocket. Toward the end of our Tonk game Norm had asked me if I play pool. He may have even mentioned One Pocket, but I was so focused on the card game that I basically blew him off. If I was half as smart as these guys, I would have gone back a day or so later and hustled him to play pool. I flew home instead. Shame on me.

AN ILL FATED TRIP

Some years later, I had made a fairly big score in real estate and was feeling very flush. The Reno pro tourney was coming up soon, so I decided that I would bring a stable of players up with me. Why not stake several players, not just one, and see how they do? I recruited Keith, Cecil Tugwell and Bill Mielke to accompany me to Reno for the winter edition of their big pool bash. I liked this tournament for the reasonable entry fee, large added money and cheap rooms. First prize was always a guaranteed $10,000, which was a nice payday back in the late 80's. Maybe one of my *horses* would knock it off.

I had just bought a very nice Dodge Ram Van conversion, with luxurious "Captain's" seats and plush carpeting throughout. It was a cozy way for the four of us to ride up to Reno. I decided that the best route was the *back* way, up Hwy. 395, along the Eastern mountain ranges of California. It was a little shorter route to Reno then going all the way up Hwy. 5 to Sacramento, and taking Hwy. 80 over the mountains. What I did not take into consideration was the weather. Living in Southern California tends to make you forget that other places have bad weather and real winters.

About halfway up to Reno the weather took a turn for the worse. It began to snow, and the road got icy and slick. I had to be very careful since I did not have snow tires or chains. We were down to a sedentary fifty mph and maybe forty on the curves in the road. I went over one hill and there was a steep downhill grade, with the road curving sharply at the bottom. I tried to slow down, but ended up missing the curve and sliding off the side of the road. We were okay, I just had to get the van straightened out and back on the icy highway. But first Cecil and Billy decided to take a quick restroom break on the side of the mountain. So we all hopped out for a minute. This was a near fatal mistake.

We had all just piled back into the van, when I looked in my rear view mirror and saw an Army truck coming down the hill. I could see the driver was fighting the steering wheel, trying to turn the truck. But it was sliding directly at us and coming fast. At the last second I yelled, "HOLD ON!" BAMMM!!! He hit us like a ton of bricks. The van was literally catapulted through the air for maybe seventy five feet, and then we slid another couple of hundred yards. Fortunately the van was facing the same direction as the truck, and he rear ended us. If we had taken a side shot, we may have all been killed.

As it was, everybody was moaning and groaning after the collision. We were all alive but in various degrees of pain. Bill and I were the lucky ones, we had been sitting in the Captain's seats which had high backs. The force of the impact had caused our bodies to break the backs of both seats, pushing them backwards and down. But those seats saved us from more serious injury. Our whiplash was aggravating, but minor compared to what Keith and Cecil went through. They got hurt, bad! Both of them were thrown around in the back of the van, bouncing off the back doors, and bumping into all the little obstructions, like the door and window handles.

"The Left Duke", Cecil Tugwell

Keith lay still for a few minutes, not saying anything. I was very worried about him. Cecil was jabbering a mile a minute, slightly hysterical. The driver of the truck came running over to us, thinking he had killed someone. I told him to call for help, IMMEDIATELY! He had a call radio in his truck and he got right on it. Within minutes two highway patrol cars arrived. The cops took one look at the van, with it's caved in back end, and called for an ambulance. Bill and I refused medical treatment, but Keith and Cecil were rushed to the hospital in Reno.

A wrecker came and picked up the van, and towed us into Reno. Bill and I road in the truck with him. He dropped us off at the Sands Casino, van and all. Lucky for me I was a member of AAA, because they paid the towing bill. Bill and I checked into the hotel, went up to the room, and passed out. We were both exhausted and sore. I woke up hours later and my entire body was hurting. I felt like I had been in a football game with the Oakland Raiders, without padding.

Then I remembered Keith and Cecil. What happened to them? I got myself up and headed over to the hospital, which was only a few blocks from the casino. I found both of them sitting in the emergency room, all bandaged up. Cecil had mostly minor injuries, but Keith sustained a wrist fracture and back injuries. I checked them out of the hospital and paid their bill, which was several hundred dollars. At least they were both alive. We headed back over to the Sands. The tournament was due to start the next day.

From the moment we walked into the tournament room, we were surrounded by well wishers. The report of the accident had been all over the news, with radio and TV stations carrying the story. They were reporting that the California State pool champion, Keith McCready, had been injured in a car accident en route to a national championship in Reno. I had given this information to the highway patrolmen, and they passed it along to the news media. All our names had been on the news, but Keith got top billing. He liked that!

Now the question was what to do about the tournament. Cecil chose not to play. Bill Mielke did play but didn't get in the money. And Keith played too, with his bandaged up hand and bad back. How he did it I don't know. He was in pain every time he shot. And yet he won matches, and finished in the top twenty four. I have to give it to Keith. He's a gamer!

Jimmy Caras, Irving Crane, Jimmy Moore, Minnesota Fats, Luther Lassiter, UJ Puckett, Willie Mosconi

THE LEGENDS OF POOL

Bill Cayton called me up one day and told me that he was putting together a televised event, featuring all the old time pool legends. He wanted my help writing bios on all the players. He had already picked Mosconi, Cranfield, Crane, Puckett, Lassiter, Fats and Jimmy Moore. He was looking for one more player to fill the bill. He asked me if there were any black champions from the past. I said sure, there was "Black Rags" (real name Robert Woods), and he lived in Los Angeles. Rags was probably the best black pool player of his generation, kind of the heir apparent to James Evans, who preceded him. Cayton asked me to find him and see if he was interested. I got in touch with Rags, and he was thrilled at the opportunity to be on television. Just like that Rags was on the show.

I did my research and wrote all the bios for Cayton, and he invited me to come and be his guest for the matches. He would foot the bill and put me up at the hotel in Atlantic City. If the television people needed any more information, I would be available to help them. Hey why not, it sounded like fun even if all these guys were slightly over the hill.

It turned out to be a very competitive event, and there was some good money on the line. $10,000 on top as I recall. Lassiter ended up winning the Legends events both years it was played. But the pool playing was only half the fun of being there. Getting to hang out again with my old buddies (and mentors) UJ Puckett and Fats was even more fun for me. One night in particular will always stick in my mind. We were hanging out in the hotel bar (their favorite spot), and both guys were telling one outrageous story after another. The conversation got around to "60 Minutes", and UJ's recent appearance on the show. UJ had been interviewed by Harry Reasoner, and Harry had followed UJ around to his favorite haunts in Fort Worth and Dallas. UJ began to tell us what good friends he and Harry had become. He said they even went fishing together, after the show had finished shooting.

Now Fatty started teasing UJ about this, asking UJ if this was one big *fish* story. UJ took offense, and said he and Harry had become real buddies during the course of the television shoot. But Fatty was relentless and continued to rib UJ about his so called *buddy*. UJ finally looked at Fats and said, "I have Harry's phone number right in my wallet, and he said to call him anytime. You want me to call him now and prove it?" Naturally Fats said sure, prove it. It was about 1 AM, and UJ had the bartender bring a phone over and plug it in at our booth. I didn't know what to think. Harry Reasoner was an icon of that era, only about the most famous newsman in the world. I tried to talk UJ out of calling him, thinking this was not a good time to wake someone up, especially Harry Reasoner. UJ made the call.

And Harry Reasoner answered the phone. Or at least that's what UJ was claiming on our end. He whispered to us that he did in fact wake Harry up. UJ thought that was very funny, and he began to tease Harry, to get him to wake up and talk to him. Finally he succeeds, and UJ informs Harry that he is down in Atlantic City (Harry was in New York) playing in a pool tournament, and sitting next to him is Minnesota Fats and Fats wants to talk to him. Before UJ hands the phone to Fats he covers the phone and whispers to us, "He's got a broad with him." UJ chuckles and hands the phone to Fatty. Fats takes over just like he's talking to an old friend, and they talk for several minutes laughing and joking.

Fatty finally ends the conversation saying, "Okay, here's UJ," and he hands the phone back to Puckett. Now UJ goes to work on Harry, inviting him to come down to Atlantic City and hang out with him and Fats. He tries to sway him saying, "Come on Harry, it will be a lot of fun," and then he says good bye, and the phone call is over. UJ now informs us that Harry

Reasoner is coming down tomorrow, just to hang out with the two of them. I find this all a little hard to believe, as I say good night and head up to bed. I don't really think Harry Reasoner, THE HARRY REASONER, is going to drop everything and come to Atlantic City, just to pal around with UJ Puckett and Minnesota Fats. How wrong I was!

UJ is scheduled to play a match early that afternoon, so I'm curious to see what kind of shape he's in, after staying up half the night. He comes strolling into the arena, arm and arm with Harry Reasoner, and leads him over to a seat in the front row to watch his match. Harry obediently takes a seat and becomes a spectator. Along with him is a gorgeous young woman, his secretary I'm sure. I'm in a semi state of shock. No doubt about it, that is Harry Reasoner sitting in the front row. I think UJ lost the match, but that was of no consequence. Afterwards, UJ and Harry and the girl all adjourn to the hotel bar, and begin a day of drinking and merry making. That evening Fats joins them and I get an invite too. I meet Mr. Reasoner and he turns out to be a regular guy, who likes to laugh, joke, tell stories and have fun. I can see why UJ likes him so much, and Harry can drink with the best of them, let me tell you. He stayed with UJ and Fats all day and well into the night before taking his leave, muttering something silly about having to go back to work the next day.

One other interesting experience I had involving Bill Cayton had to do with Mike Tyson. Bill and his partner Jimmy Jacobs were Tyson's first managers. They hooked him up with Cus D'Amato, who had been the trainer for Rocky Marciano, and together they were molding Tyson into a contender. Tyson was fighting one night at Resorts Hotel in Atlantic City, and I was back there directing the Last Call For Nine Ball, also being held at Resorts. Bill Staton, aka Weenie Beenie, had hired me to help him run the show. Pat Fleming was there as well, so we had a good crew. We needed it, with no less than 357 players!

They were actually filming some scenes at Resorts for *The Color Of Money*, and Paul Newman was there for the film shoot. One afternoon I was up on the directors podium with Bill Staton, and a couple of hotel security guards came up the steps. They cleared everyone off the podium except Billy and me. I wasn't sure what was going on, because I was right in the middle of introducing the players for the next round, so I couldn't really look around. During my introductions some guy sits down right in between Billy and me. What is going on I'm thinking, but I continue with my intros. When I finish I look to my left, and stare into the crystal blue eyes of Paul Newman. He smiles at me and asks,

"Which table is Sigel on?" He had come over to watch his friend and coach Mike Sigel play. So Paul sat there between Billy and me watching Sigel's match, until they called him on the walkie-talkie, and told him they were ready for more filming.

But let's get back to Mike Tyson. He is still an unknown fighter, and his name means nothing to me. The good news is the fight is being held in the Superstar Ballroom, directly across the hall from where the pool tournament is going on. Bill Cayton has come over to the tournament, and personally invited me to watch the fight. I told him that I was a little busy right now, but if he sends someone over to get me, I will take a break and join him for a few minutes. He tells me that Tyson's fights usually only take a few minutes. I wonder what he meant by that. Oh well, I'm back at it, and sure enough a guy comes to the podium and asks for me. He says to come with him, that Bill Cayton is waiting for me across the hall. I tell Pat that I'll be back shortly, I'm taking a break. No problem he says.

I'm escorted into the ballroom, and led to a large booth that sits ringside. In the booth are Cayton and Jacobs and their wives. I join them, and Bill tells me that Tyson's fight is up next. Sure enough, a minute or so later a very large man enters the ring. An impressive specimen I thought. No, I'm told that is not Mike Tyson. Another minute goes by, and a much smaller man comes into the ring. He takes off his robe, and I immediately notice his huge thighs, as big around as my waist. He is a short, compact man with a sinister look on his face. The face of a killer. This is TYSON! There are quick introductions for this fight, a prelim. It is only Mike's fifth fight I am told. He has won the rest by knockouts, none going past the second round. Hmmm, this should be interesting.

The fight begins with the usual sparring around. The big guy throws a few jabs Mike's way, and he brushes them off. It doesn't look like Tyson is doing anything but bobbing around. Suddenly he throws a huge punch that catches the bigger man square in the chest, above his heart. BOOM! The sound of the blow is a loud clap, like a batter launching a home run ball. The big guy drops to the canvas, immobilized. He can't move, or breathe for that matter. He is counted out, but remains motionless on the canvas. I've never seen a knockout like this, one blow to the chest. Finally the guy is assisted to his feet. He is in acute pain, and a doctor attends to him. I say my good byes, stunned by the Godzilla like knockout I have just witnessed.

Maybe thirty minutes later, Cayton brings Tyson over to the pool tournament, and they walk up the steps to the podium. He introduces Mike to me and I extend my hand. In a high pitched voice Mike says, "Hi, I'm Mike." I'm surprised by the effeminate voice of this cold blooded killer, but I respond to him, "Congratulations Mike, I hope you'll be a good champion some day." Somehow, I knew even then that this man was destined to be the World Champion one day.

The incomparable UJ Puckett

Jimmy Moore showing the crowd how it's done.

A happy Willie Mosconi with Bill Cayton (after beating Fats).

PROMOTING (PT. 2)

My biggest promotions were yet to come. In 1992 I put together the first Los Angeles Open 9-Ball Championship. I accomplished this by enlisting the support of twenty four people who each kicked in $2,500 to $5,000. I put in about 25K of my own. The tournament was held at the Burbank Hilton Convention Center, a beautiful facility with lots of room. Inside we constructed two arenas side by side, with four tables in the center of each one. Elevated bleachers nine rows high surrounded each arena, with seating for approximately 750 people; 1,500 total in both arenas. It was a wonderful set up, with easy viewing for the four tables down below, and a spectator could move from one arena to the other to watch matches.

Outside in the expansive lobby nearly forty vendors were selling billiards merchandise. We got some terrific publicity thanks to my media director David Thomson. We had television coverage on no less than five local stations, and one station even did their evening sports report from the floor of the pool tournament. In addition, we placed ads in the Los Angeles Times and several other major newspapers in Southern California. Guess what, it worked! The tournament was crowded each day and we had huge crowds on the weekend, selling well over 1,000 tickets on Friday and Saturday.

We had a men's division with sixty four players and a $100,000 purse, plus a women's division with thirty two players playing for another $40,000. The men and women played side by side all week long and the fans loved it. ESPN covered the tourney and televised both final matches. Barry Tompkins did commentary along with Mike Sigel. Earl won the men's final over CJ Wiley, and Peg Ledman won the women's over JoAnn Mason Parker. Earl got $21,000 for first and CJ won $11,000 for second. Peg won $10,000 and JoAnn got $6,000. Big pay outs for 1992!

All and all a great event, or so I thought. The players and the new tour commissioner Don Mackey all congratulated me on holding such a successful event. Less than two weeks later I got a call from Mackey. He began by congratulating me again, and then informed me that if I wanted to do this event next year I cannot have a women's division. I thought he was joking since doing it this way attracted a lot of media attention. Sure enough the next day Allen Hopkins (the men's association President) called me and explained that the men would no longer play alongside the women. He said that the men were the best players and deserved to get the recognition, not the women. A bit chauvinistic and very short sighted.

I was floored by their attitude. I had just put on the best tournament of the year (Earl said it was the best tournament ever), and now they were now telling me I can't do it again the following year. Talk about shooting yourself in the foot. I had produced the L.A. Open as a prototype event that could be duplicated by promoters in other major cities. It could have been the beginning of a major pool tour. Instead it brought an end to the alliance between the men and the women. After this happened the women started their own separate tour, now known as the Women's Professional Billiard Tour. It has thrived while the men have continued to struggle. Shame on them, it was their own fault and it wouldn't be the last time they would blow it big time.

A few months later at the BCA Trade Show in Las Vegas; Mackey, Hopkins and Bob Meucci called all the major pool promoters together for a meeting. There were about ten to twelve of us in attendance. Mackey led off by telling us these tournaments we had been producing no longer belonged to us. He said they all belonged to the Men's Professional Billiard Association, and if they wanted to let us continue to produce them they would. It was a whole new ball game. The MPBA was now our *partner* and would share 50-50 in all revenues generated. Mackey had seen the big gate we did in Los Angeles and all the vendors paying for their space, and he wanted a piece of the action. We were being "muscled", for lack of a better word.

What Mackey and his confederates didn't realize was that producing major pool tournaments was not a money making proposition. I had lost money at the inaugural Los Angeles Open. We had over $120,000 in expenses ($60,000 alone in added money) and only about $100,000 in receipts. I asked him if he wanted to share in the losses as well. All the promoters laughed at this remark, but Mackey and friends didn't think it was that funny. Don Mackey effectively killed all hopes for a professional pool tour in America that day. There was not one promoter in that room who would go along with such an outrageous proposal. What he was asking us to do was to put up ALL the money to stage the event, and then split the proceeds with the MPBA (him). It was a guaranteed financial disaster this way and we all knew it.

The following year I staged a second L.A. Open, only this time it was an all around event with three divisions. It was not "sanctioned" by the MPBA, and most of their players boycotted the tournament. That meant that most of the top name players didn't play, including many players who had been my friends for years. I realized then there was no loyalty in this game. It was a valuable lesson for me. A few of the players did cross the picket line and play, along with just about every pool hustler on the continent. We had big fields and even bigger prize money, paying out over $160,000. Mark Tadd won $27,000 alone! Once again I lost money and decided that producing major pro tournaments was not the ticket, especially with the current leadership in men's professional pool.

I had already petitioned the BCA to produce a major amateur 9-Ball event, since they already had a very successful Eight Ball tourney each year. They accepted my proposal and this is how the North American 9-Ball Championships came to be. The BCA stuck with me for a few years and then they pulled the plug on their sponsorship. I was left high and dry until the Sands Regency Casino in Reno came to the rescue. They would put up $20,000 in added money if I would relocate the tournament to their facility. At the Sands the event became known as The U.S. Bar Table Championships. It got bigger and better each year and after thirteen years I sold it to Mark Griffin, owner of the BCA pool leagues. The tournament had gone full circle.

I would be derelict if I didn't mention my good fortune sponsoring players in the U.S. Bar Table Championships. I put Danny Medina in a few times and he always made money. His girlfriend Laurette also helped us out, along with Chris MacDonald's wife Barbara, who handled the tournament boards for years. One year Danny even won the Eight Ball division and we chopped up $5,000. But the best horse I had in this event was definitely Cliff Joyner. The first year I staked him he won both divisions plus a $1,000 Bonus. Our take was $11,000 and I got half. Cliff took his share down to the casino floor and promptly blew it. He came up to my room at eight in the morning and asked for $300 to get home on. Easy come easy go, but that's the life of a gambler.

RONNIE ALLEN VS. DANNY DILIBERTO

I got the idea to record pool matches at the Sands Regency tournament in 1987. I thought that many pool fans who couldn't make it to Reno might enjoy seeing some great players in action. So what I did was hire a local television production company to work with me. They normally shot local TV commercials, but were quite willing to bring their equipment to the Sands and record a pool match. I spent one day with the crew prepping them for the show, doing my best to explain how we should cover the matches. They were all ears and eager to go.

I invited Pat Fleming to do commentary with me, and we recorded the final three matches of the tournament. Featured players included Ron Rosas, Allen Hopkins, Mike Sigel and David Howard. They turned out to be three terrific matches and I sold VHS copies of them through the national billiard media. They were best sellers and my initial run of 150 videos was gone in a month or so. I eventually sold about 500 tapes total at $20 a tape, not bad money in those days. I still have DVD copies of these early matches and occasionally someone will inquire about obtaining them. They contain classic footage of these players in their prime.

A couple of months later Pat Fleming called me and asked if I was planning to record the final matches of the Rak 'M Up Classic in Columbia, SC. I hadn't really thought about it, and it was all the way across the country. So I told him I was going to pass on this one. He asked me if I cared if he did it. I told him to go right ahead, I thought that would be a good thing. That tournament was the beginning of Accu-Stats Video Productions.

I liked the idea of producing pool shows and selling the tapes, since there was so little pool on regular television. But there weren't many pool tournaments on the West Coast at the time, and I didn't want to keep doing the Sands over and over again. That's when Elliot Robbins came back into my life. Little Elliot was a pool hustler I met years before at Ye Billiard Den in Hollywood. He was from New Jersey and was a fair little shortstop. I hadn't seen him in years until we met again in Marina del Rey, CA.

Turns out we were living in the same apartment complex and I ran into him in the 'rec' center. They had six tables set up there and I would go practice from time to time. Elliot was trying to hustle the residents there, and someone brought me down there to play him. We got a big laugh when we saw each other, and began reminiscing about the good old days. He asked me about Ronnie Allen, who had been his hero, and I told him Ronnie was spending more time at the track then in the poolroom. Too bad he said, because he had money now and would love to put Ronnie in action. I told him that might be possible because Danny Diliberto had been woofing at Ronnie to play. Danny was the general manager of the biggest poolroom in Phoenix, a place called the Golden Eight Ball.

Elliot said, "Let's get it on then," just like that. And that's how the World One Pocket Challenge Match came to be. I contacted Ronnie and he said sure he would play Danny, anytime and anywhere. Elliot was willing to stake him in a $10,000 match, and Ronnie loved the sound of that. Why

Ronnie "Fast Eddie" Allen

Danny Diliberto

not, it was a free roll for $5,000. I called Danny and asked him if he would like to play Ronnie a $10,000 match in his poolroom. Sure he said, bring him over. We had a game! All along my idea was to record this epic match and sell the tapes.

I hired a local video production company that was willing to send a crew over to Phoenix and do the shoot. The budget would be $4,000 for the three days, plus all their expenses. Done deal! Danny would be staked by David Lee, who owned the poolroom, and Ronnie had Elliot in his corner. Ronnie prepared for the match by playing Jack Cooney some fifty a game One Pocket. A few sessions with Jack and Ronnie was back in "dead stroke". Meanwhile, Danny was working out every day on the Centennial table in the "pit" at the Golden Eight Ball.

Things were rolling good for me back then. I had just refinanced my home and pulled $50,000 out on my end, so I had a little extra *do re mi*. Harry Platis had been bugging me to play some high dollar One Hole, and now I had some *ammo*. He had been hustling me to play for over two years, and I kept telling him he had no chance with me. That only made him more anxious to play. We had *practiced* some 9-Ball a year or so earlier at Caesar's Palace. I was the tournament director and had gone down early in the morning to open up the room for practice. Harry was the first one through the doors and he asked me to practice with him for $25 a game. I told him he couldn't win but he didn't seem to care. Two hours later I had relieved him of $400. Now he was after me to play $1,000 a game One Pocket. He figured I would dog it for that amount. And the truth be known I was apprehensive about betting that high. I never had before.

But now I was sitting on some serious money and could handle the big bet. Harry called me and said he would be coming over to Phoenix with Keith. Would I like to play some One Pocket? Once again I told him he couldn't beat me. He replied that he thought I would dog it for the cash. Okay I said, I'll play. And we did play, for $1,000 a game. More about that later.

The big match between Ronnie and Danny went off as scheduled, and it turned out to be a doozy. They played three out of five sets, each set a race to five. The money was secured in the office safe, all $20,000 of it! I saw it with my own eyes. This was a real match for real money, so don't let anyone tell you otherwise. The match went down to the final set, tied at two sets each. Both players desperately wanted to win this match and the money and prestige that went with it. The place was packed all three days and there were many side bets being wagered as well. I acted as the director on the

Pat Fleming, creator of Accu-Stats Video Productions.
An excellent player in his own right.

shoot, switching cameras to record the best angle on every shot. In the end Ronnie got there and Danny was crestfallen. He went into his private office and would not emerge for hours.

Best of all we had the whole thing on tape, all ten hours of it. It became a best seller and still sells even to this day. As for me and Harry, we had our One Pocket match for $1,000 a game. It started on the first night, after Ronnie and Danny had completed their first set. Harry and I played on the same table, and he won the flip and got to break first. I lost that game and was stuck $1,000. I was a little sick to my stomach, and knew I had to win the second game on my break. It was a close game, but I got there and began to feel more comfortable with the bet. I won the next six games in a row before Harry pulled up for the night.

The next night Ronnie insisted that we play partners against Harry and Keith. Bad idea! We lost two games fast at $1,000 a pop before I quit. I had lost back $1,000 (500 a game) of the money I'd won the night before, and played horribly with Ronnie as my partner. He was sharking me every time it was my shot, telling me not to shoot the shot I liked, and to go for something else instead. It wasn't working and I pulled up fast.

Now Harry and I resumed our match and I got him for four more games this time. We were done, but I had made my biggest pool score ever. When I got home I bought myself a beautiful truck thanks to my friend Harry Platis. We did play again a few more times. The next time was for $500 a game and I won another $2,500. Then we played at the Sands for $200 a game, after I told Harry I would only *practice* with him. He insisted we bet something and I won a grand. Years went by and Harry improved. The next time we played was also at the Sands. It was a race to four for $1,000 and Harry won. He played good too. A few years after that we played once more at Derby City. This time it was a race to five in Banks. Harry won again on the case ball at 4-4 in games and 4-4 in the final game. He beat me for another grand. It looks like Harry is the better man today, so I may have to leave him alone.

THE GREAT CUE RECOVERIES

I already told you about Keith's big win at the B.C. Open when he (and I) won $25,000. What I didn't tell you was that he was using my prized Szamboti, that I loaned him for the tournament. He had come by my house a week or so before the tournament looking for a cue to shoot with. I showed him three or four good cues but he wasn't satisfied with any of them. He spotted my Szamboti sitting in the case and asked, "What about that cue?" "No way," I said, "That's my prize Szamboti." "Well let me check it out anyway," he pleaded. So I let him *check it out*. Much to my dismay Keith decided that was the cue he HAD to have. I reluctantly let him borrow it.

The rest is history, or so they like to say. He did win the tournament using my cue but that was not the end of the story. Keith had a long-standing debt with a New York based player, known as "Steve The Whale". Steve was a monster, well over six feet tall and in excess of four hundred pounds. Steve came to the B.C. Open and asked Keith to make good on the old debt. Keith responded that he had a backer and had to straighten up with him first. But Steve had other plans. He went to the front desk and convinced a clerk that he was Keith McCready, and was locked out of his room. The clerk had a bellman let Steve into the room, and then he made off with my cue.

So Keith returns triumphantly to Los Angeles, minus my Szamboti. I wanted to kill him, but since he had just won 25K, I held off doing any bodily harm. A Szamboti then was worth maybe $1,000, so I was still way ahead on the deal. I was mad as Hell but figured what could I do. Keith knew The Whale had stolen the cue, but he was powerless to do anything about it. He agreed to *work it off* for me; meaning that his next winnings would go toward repaying me for the lost cue. I accepted this because I felt there was nothing else I could do. The Whale and my Szamboti were in New York, and I was not about to fly across the country looking for him.

Along comes "Brooklyn Butch". Butch was a notorious East Coast tush hog (tough guy) who had taken a liking to me years before, when he saw me challenging all the champions in 7/11. He told me later that he loved the fact that I never asked for weight and played all the best players in New York. The fact that I got trimmed didn't enter into the equation in his mind. Anyway, Butch had learned that The Whale had stolen my prized Szamboti. It helped that Butch was a cue collector, who appreciated a well made cue. He was also a personal friend of Gus Szamboti's, and it didn't sit well with him to hear one of his cues had been stolen.

A week or so after the B.C. Open concluded I get a call from Butch, now living in Glendale, California. He congratulates me on booking a winner with Keith and then inquired about my Szamboti. "Did Keith use your Szamboti," he asks me. "Yes," I reply. "Did he bring it back with him?" he asks. "Well, no he didn't." "Do you know what happened to it?" I was beginning to realize that Butch knew the whole story, and was only calling me for confirmation. How he found out I have no idea, and don't to this day. Let's just say he has pretty good connections in New York.

Out of the blue Butch asks me if I want my cue back. Of course I tell him, I would like my cue back! He tells me to come to his shop that evening and we'll do something about it. I had serious doubts about all this but I went anyway. I got there about 7 PM and Butch starts telling me about his history with Steve, the guy who stole my cue. He explains that Steve is deathly afraid of him and will do anything he asks. With that he calls The Golden Cue in Queens, New York. Butch asks for Steve The Whale, and soon enough he comes to the phone. I can only hear one side of the conversation, but it went something like this;

"Hello Steve, this is Butch."
"Uh huh, uh huh."
"I heard you got Keith's cue."
Silence.......
Louder now, "DON'T LIE TO ME STEVE!"
Pause.....
"Okay that's better."
"Did you know that cue belongs to a friend of mine, Jay Helfert?"
Long pause.......
"It does matter to me! I told you he's a friend of mine. A good friend!"
Another pause.....
"I want you to send that cue back tomorrow! To me!"
Pauseeeeeeee
"I'm not kidding Steve, I want it NOW!"..............
"You don't want me to come back there and visit you do you? I will you know."....................
"If I have to come back there you aren't going to like it! You do know what's going to happen don't you?" ....
"Okay that's more like it.....get a pen and write down my address."

Three days later Butch called to tell me he had my cue. Delivered by UPS. Swear to God!

This second story occurred about eight years ago, when Tang Hoa was still active as a pro player. I was the tournament director for the Hard Times Jamboree being held in Sacramento, and Tang drove up with me to play. The year before he had snapped off both the One Pocket and 9-Ball divisions, and won nearly six grand. Lucky me had a piece.

There was considerable action at Hard Times, and that always interested Tang, so he hung out all night hoping to catch someone. One night he fell asleep in the bleachers with his cue by his side. When he woke up the cue was gone. I got to the poolroom that morning to prepare for the tournament, and Tang was there waiting, anxious to tell me about his missing cue. He had reconciled himself to the fact his cue was gone and wasn't coming back. I made him tell me the whole story, exactly where he was in the bleachers, what time he slept until, etc. I knew Chuck and Mike (the owners) had video cameras throughout Hard Times and I wanted to see what I could find on the tapes.

When Mike got in I related the story to him and showed him where Tang had been sleeping. Mike said there was a camera above the back door that had a view of the bleacher area. Into the office we go to review the tape. Sure enough we see Tang laying on the bleachers with the cue propped up by his head. We fast forward through the tape for a long time and all of sudden there is a blur, and the cue is gone! We slow down the tape, and you can see a guy pick up the cue and move quickly away. It is too grainy to make out his face, but we can clearly see him grab the cue.

Next we go to the tape of the camera by the front entrance. Everyone enters and exits this way. It isn't so hard to find the guy on this tape. We know what time he stole the cue from the other tape. Mike fiddles with the tape a moment, and then he finds the guy walking near the entrance with Tang's cue by his side. You can clearly see the logo on the side of the case. It is a nice Jack Justis case with the name Tang "Hold 'em" Hoa on the side. There are two Aces embroidered next to his name; clearly identifiable.

This is a much better view of the guy, but I have no idea who he is. We decide to ask some of the locals, who are more familiar with everyone in the area, to take a look at the tape. We call in Chris MacDonald and Dave Piona. Bingo, Dave knows the guy! He is from San Francisco and has even backed Dave a time or two. Dave tells us that the guy has only been around for a few months, and he doesn't know him that well, but he does have his phone number. I ask Dave to call him and inquire about the missing cue. Don't accuse him of anything, just suggest maybe he made a mistake. Oh, and let him know we have him on tape.

Dave gets the guy on the phone and naturally he denies any knowledge of Tang's cue. I ask Dave to let me talk with him, and he hands me the phone. My tone is not nearly so friendly. I tell the guy we have everything on tape, and if he doesn't do the right thing we're calling the cops and turning the tape over to them. It's a total bluff, the tape is too grainy to see much more than the cue case and a vague look at the guy holding it. The guy sounds worried but continues to deny any knowledge of the missing cue. I tell him he has exactly twenty four hours to return the cue! I don't know if this will work or not. I end the conversation by telling him to think about the consequences.

Less than an hour later Dave comes rushing over to me. He says the guy just called him and confessed to having Tang's cue. He says he made a mistake and grabbed the wrong cue when he was leaving. Right!!! He wants to return it but is afraid he will be arrested. I tell Dave to call him back and set up a rendezvous somewhere besides Hard Times. Tell him he will meet him alone. Dave calls him back and they agree to meet at the IHOP a mile or so away. It's a long drive from the Bay area to Sacramento, so they agree to meet there in two hours. Two hours later Dave heads for the IHOP. Thirty minutes or so after that he returns with Tang's cue. Tang and his cue (and case) are reunited. Another happy ending!

Our last little tale has to do with my dear friend Ming Ng. She was staying with me in Venice at the time and was playing on the Women's Pro Tour. This was back in 2001 or maybe 2002. I got a line on an inexpensive condo for sale in Santa Monica and we went to take a look at it. It was about mid day and we were going to play some pool afterward, so she took her cue. We were in my Ford Bronco II, and we found a parking space right in front of the building. We hopped out, made sure to lock all the doors and went to see the condo. The cue was resting comfortably in back.

We went inside, and spent considerable time checking the place out and talking prices with the agent. Maybe forty five minutes went by before we left. We were met by the sight of my beautiful little Bronco with a smashed in side window. The car had been looted, my new stereo had been ripped from the dash, and Ming's cue was gone. BUMMER!

Tang Hoa, 1998 U.S. Open Runner-Up

"The Empress" Ming Ng, former WPBA Touring Pro

I called the cops and made a police report, and they assured me they would be in contact with the local pawn shops. We drove around to every poolroom in the area and let them know about the theft as well. Then we went home in a funky mood. I sat there just thinking about it. What could I do? This was Ming's Predator playing cue and her break cue, plus the cool case Jack Justis had made for her. It said "Empress Ming" on the side in bold letters.

I had been informed by the cops that this was *the* bad neighborhood in Santa Monica, infested by crack heads. No wonder the price on the condo was so good. I had an idea though. These guys needed money to buy their drugs. They would have trouble unloading the cues in the fancy case. It was too easily identifiable. I would offer a reward, "No Questions Asked!" I made up a reward flyer on my computer. It said "$200 REWARD" in bold letters on the top. And then, "Missing Cue, No Questions Asked for its safe return." I added a description of the cues and the case, and my phone number. I made about eight to ten copies of the flyer, and went back and posted them in the same area where we got heisted.

Ming was very hesitant about all this. She thought I could get jumped and maybe beat up. I told her not to worry, these guys only want money, not me. I posted the flyers all over the neighborhood, particularly around the liquor store on the corner. That looked like a likely hang out for dealers and their customers. Then I went back home and waited. Lo and behold, I got a call about eight that evening. It was a guy claiming to work for the city sanitation department. He said he found a cue case in a dumpster. We talked briefly and then he hung up. I think he was afraid of the call being traced. He said he would call me back later. Maybe he just needed more time to get his story straight.

Sure enough an hour or so later he calls me back. I have him describe the case to me. It's Ming's, no question about it. He tells me I must come by myself to pick it up, and then he gives me the address. It's one block away from the condo we went to look at earlier. It's now after 9 PM and Ming does not want me to go there alone. I refuse to take her along. It could queer the whole deal. I load my .25 and put it in the back pocket of my jeans. They won't be robbing me!

As I pull up near the address I notice two guys across the street eyeing my Bronco. My instincts tell me these are the actual thieves, observing from a distance. They are making sure I'm alone. I park and walk to the small duplex. The front door is covered with a heavy metal gate. I knock once with no answer. I'm getting uncomfortable and keeping an eye on the two guys across the street. If they even move toward me the gun is coming out, and it's cocked and loaded with seven little daggers. I will definitely use it if necessary.

I knock once more, louder this time. Someone opens the door a crack. "I came to pick up the cue," I tell him. "Do you have the money?" he asks me. "Yes," I reply. The gate is still closed, only the door is open a hair. Now he brings the case to the door for me to see. "Open it," I say. "I want to see the cues inside." He does and they are both there. He opens the gate, I hand him the $200, and he gives me the case. I'm out of there and back in my car quick. As I drive off I look in my rear view mirror. The two guys are walking across the street in the direction of the apartment I just left. They're heading over to chop up the money I'm sure. But I got Ming's cues, and that's all I cared about.

"The Empress" and her prized cue

THE CHALLENGE OF CHAMPIONS

In 1991, my friend Matt Braun got the idea to hold a tournament that featured the eight best pool players in the world, playing "Winner Take All" for $50,000. He wanted to produce an event with the biggest first prize in pool. Matt called me and asked if I would come to Vegas and direct the tournament for him. He was willing to pay me a nice fee, and that always had a way of persuading me.

This first time event was held at the Mirage Hotel and featured an all star cast; Mike Sigel, Buddy Hall, Earl Strickland, Allen Hopkins, David Howard, Nick Varner, Jim Rempe and Mike Lebron. All premier players! This was a "made for television" event, to be featured on ESPN. The Mirage made a big deal out of this tournament, and even announced it on their giant billboard. The guy in charge of the sports book decided to make a line on the event, so spectators could bet on the players. He installed Sigel and Hall as the favorites, and made them 3-1 to win the whole thing. The other players got various lines like 4-1, 5-1 and 6-1 in David Howard's case. All good so far.

Mike Lebron was made a 20-1 *dog*. Why, I have no idea. He had as much chance of winning as anyone else. They were short matches and he was a great 9-Ball player. The players got wind of what was going on, and the unusual *line* made on Lebron. They knew it didn't make sense for anyone to be a 20-1 underdog in a field of only eight players, especially a top player like Lebron. What happened next I can't verify with any proof, other than to say that I was a witness to the whole thing. And things got funny real fast.

The betting limit on this event was $200, and none of the players were allowed to make a bet. But they had friends along with them, and there was nothing to stop them from placing a bet, if you get my drift. Seems like there were a bunch of $200 bets made on Lebron before the odds suddenly dropped to 10-1. The betting tapered off after that. Mike cruised into the finals without much difficulty, and the other players seemed just as delighted with his success as he was.

Now he had to beat Buddy Hall in the finals. It was an excellent match with good play on the part of both players, although Buddy missed a ball or two that maybe he shouldn't have. I had the best seat in the house, ringside, racking the balls and refereeing.

It came down to the case game, the winner getting the Fifty Grand! Buddy got the first shot at an open table, ran down to the six ball and played shape for a combination on the nine. He could have just as easily tried to get position to make the six cleanly, but he didn't choose that option. He was fairly close to the six ball and the nine was maybe a foot or so away, and about a diamond from the corner pocket. It wasn't a cinch by any means, but it was a combo that Buddy was a favorite to make. Except this time he missed it badly, hitting on the wrong side of the nine ball. It almost appeared that he missed it purposely, but like I said, I can't say for sure. I'm only a witness and you know how eye witnesses are, unreliable at best. Mike got out from there and was jubilant in victory, as well he should be.

I heard later that there were only a dozen or so tickets sold on Mike for $200 each. At 20-1, that would make the total payoff around $50,000. A bad day for the sports book, but I guess it could have been a lot worse. Needless to say that was the last year the book made a line on the Challenge Of Champions. As far as the $50,000 prize goes, I'm not so sure that all went to Mike either. Let's see, a seven way chop (if one player refused) would still leave over $7,000 apiece. I'm just speculating here naturally. Not casting any aspersions, although the following year the players had to sign an agreement saying no deals of any kind would be made. In the event of deal making, the promoter (Matt Braun) could now refuse payment of the fifty thousand.

Allen Hopkins, 1993 Winner of the Challenge of Champions

EARL'S TEN RACKS

Another famous event in pool that I witnessed was when Earl ran the ten racks for a million dollars. Here's the way it all came down.

CJ Wiley, Earl Strickland and several other players decided to break away from Don Mackey and the MPBA and start their own pro tour. CJ called this fledgling group the Professional Cuesports Association (PCA). To create interest in his new tour, CJ decided to offer a million dollar prize to anyone running ten consecutive racks of 9-Ball, and he called this The Million Dollar Challenge. This would be insured in a similar fashion to the Hole In One prizes in golf tournaments. So he contacted the appropriate insurance companies and inquired about buying insurance.

Meanwhile the first PCA event was scheduled in Dallas at CJ's Billiards, a very nice billiard room that he owned. I was hired to direct along with John McChesney and Robin Adair. The room had twenty four Gold Crown tables, and they all had fairly tight pockets. There was little chance of anyone running ten racks here, or so we thought.

The night before the tourney was to begin I met CJ's insurance man in the office of the poolroom. They were ironing out the details of the Million Dollar offering. At this time CJ made the initial payment on the insurance policy, even though a formal document did not exist yet. According to accepted insurance law, the policy was in force the moment money was paid and accepted.

The next day the tournament began, and no one was running any racks, let alone ten! I think the high run of the day was three racks. That evening, Earl began his second match on a back table with Nick Mannino. We were playing *Rack Your Own*, and Earl had figured out the best way to rack on this table.

He was able to make the nine ball move toward the corner pocket on nearly every break. He won the flip and ran the first five racks, making two nine balls on the break. At this point they called me over to rack the balls. One of the stipulations of the insurance policy was that after a player runs five racks, a referee must rack the balls from then on for everything to be legal.

I hurried back to the table, and Earl was already racking the balls for game six. I said to him, "Hold it Earl, I have to rack." Nothing doing, Earl wouldn't let me touch the rack. He quickly finishes racking and breaks the balls, making a ball. The nine ball moves slowly toward the corner pocket and stops. He then runs out in his usual fast and loose style. CJ's wife Angela is now on the scene with her video camera, recording everything. That is another stipulation of the insurance policy. The final five racks must be recorded on tape.

Now CJ and I are imploring Earl to let me rack, explaining to him that if he doesn't let me rack it will cancel the potential million dollar award. Earl finally relents and lets me rack the balls. I clean the table with my hands, trying to insure a good tight rack. I see that Earl has figured out a breaking pattern on this table, and I want to nullify that advantage. The nine barely moves this time, but Earl makes a ball and runs out anyway. Same thing in racks eight and nine. He needs to run one more rack for $1,000,000! Oh my God!

I'm a little nervous myself, and I make sure to put a really tight rack up there. Once again Earl delivers a powerful break and balls fly everywhere. One ball goes down and the nine ends up about a foot or so from the corner pocket. Not really that close. The cue ball has been kicked down near the end rail, and the one ball is up by the side pocket. All three balls are on the same side of the table. Earl has a few options here. He can try to shoot the one down in the corner past the nine, or he can try a long combination from the one to the nine. Either way it's a difficult shot, and he spends quite a bit of time examining the table.

Finally Earl decides to go for all the marbles, the long difficult combination. Even for a great player like Earl, he's an underdog to make this shot. Maybe one out of five times he will make it. Earl gets down and fires hard, perhaps hoping to luck something in if he misses the nine. The one flies towards the nine and makes a perfect hit. THE NINE GOES IN! EARL HAS WON A **MILLION DOLLARS**! Or has he? For good measure Earl runs the next rack, for eleven consecutive racks. It's a Race To Thirteen, so the match isn't quite over yet. Nick may have won a game or two after that, but it made little difference. Earl has run ten racks and the entire crowd has witnessed it.

After the match ends a petition is passed around for people to sign, saying they had witnessed the whole thing from beginning to end. By the time I signed off as the referee there must have been twenty five or thirty signatures on that sheet. A small table was then brought out, and a stack of Earls photo's was placed on it. Earl sat down at the table and signed a photo for every fan who wanted one. He didn't just sign his signature either. He wrote, "To 'So and So', The night I ran ten racks for $1,000,000, Earl Strickland." Pretty cool I thought. Why I didn't have him sign one for me I have no idea. There must have been over a hundred people who lined up at that table, and it took Earl a good hour or two to give each of them a signed photo. I really admired Earl for doing that.

Afterwards, Earl and I headed back to the hotel in the same van. I told him how proud I was of him for his achievement, and also for taking the time to sign all those photos for his fans. Then I asked him the one burning question in my mind. "What were you thinking when you got down to shoot that long combination on the nine for all the money?" Earl paused a moment, looked at me and said, "I just wanted to give it a legitimate chance." I'll never forget that remark from an all time great player.

Now the plot thickened. The insurance companies (including Lloyds of London) who underwrote the policy were balking at making payment. It did look bad. CJ takes out the policy, and the first day of the tournament someone runs ten racks! Interestingly enough, no one has done anything like that since in a major pool tournament. Efren may have run nearly nine full racks in a comeback win at the World Pool Championships one year. That's the most I remember off the top of my head.

CJ went ahead and made the initial $50,000 payment to Earl out of his own pocket. That took a lot of class. He didn't want to look like a welsher, or make the PCA look phony. The insurance pay out of the million dollars was an Annuity, structured at $50,000 a year for twenty years. Still not bad, like a twenty year pension. Except they didn't want to pay anything. They were trying to say no policy was in effect yet. That became the key question; Did CJ make an initial payment, and was it accepted by the agent?

It all became a matter for attorneys and the courts to settle. The whole mess took two years to sort out, but finally the insurance companies made a settlement. Earl got a lump sum, something like $250,000. And CJ got his $50,000 back. Earl was happy and so was CJ. To this day, CJ has never done anything with the video of the last five games that Angela recorded. I think it would be a best seller.

Earl and Sigel, two of the greatest in their prime

Earl learning from the Master, Buddy Hall.

BEATING THE CRAP OUT OF THE SANDS

Back in the days when I was running the Sands Reno tourney, there were big fields and most of the champions came out to play. Players like Sigel, Hall, Reyes, Strickland, Rempe and Davenport used to win this one. For me it was ten long grueling days, with a four day amateur tournament prior to the main event. At the end of the tournament I got paid, and like many of the players, I put some of my hard earned cheese in action at the Sands.

The pool players were real gamblers, looking to bet it up whenever possible. Guys like Keith and Grady were a threat to make a score at any time. The casino bosses were very much aware of this. One year, maybe it was 1991 or '92, a bunch of us hit the lone crap table at the Sands on the night the tourney concluded. I remember Jimmy Mataya and Nick Varner were in the game along with some West Coast players. About eight or nine of us surrounded the table and got the game rolling. I started out betting $5 chips and taking $10 odds. The bigger gamblers like Mataya and Varner were betting $25 and taking $50 odds.

Well, the dice got hot and stayed hot. The first guy to roll held the dice for close to thirty minutes, and made 15-20 passes, plus loads of good numbers. We were all getting pumped up. By the end of his roll, I was betting quarter chips and taking $50 odds. Mataya and Varner were betting all black ($100 chips), as were a couple of other guys. The second *roller* also got hot and made a dozen passes or so. Oh my God, we were on a major heater here. Now it was my turn, and sure enough I threw about ten passes, and held the dice for quite a while. We were killing the Sands crap table, and they had to call for a *refill*, meaning to bring in more money. We were in the process of busting the house!

Now it was Nicky's turn, and it was more of the same. We kept right on winning and screaming at the top of our lungs. A big crowd had gathered around the table to witness the slaughter. The lambs were killing the lions! The table limits were only $200 with double odds, meaning the most money you could lay on any one number was $600 ($200 in front and $400 in back). No matter, Mataya and Varner and one or two others were betting the limit, and taking more than one number. Finally Nicky crapped out, but not before we made another killing. Now it was Mataya's turn, our 'de facto' ringleader.

Everybody loaded up on the pass line, and Jimmy gave the dice a heave. SEVEN! We all went crazy, with Jimmy the loudest and craziest of the bunch. You could hear him across the street. The pit bosses and the crap dealers were looking uncomfortable as they paid us off. I could see the grumbling going on between the bosses as they watched us rake in the chips. Reluctantly they pushed the dice back to Jimmy. He picked out two good ones and let fly again. ELEVEN! Winner! Winner! Winner! Collectively there was a shout that could be heard all over Reno.

Now a strange thing happened, which I have never seen before or since in any other casino. The "Box Man" (he sits in the center of the dice table), who controls the game, would not pass the dice back to Jimmy. He took the five dice and passed them to the next guy after Jimmy. He wanted this guy to reach down and pick out two dice to roll with. Jimmy was getting passed up on his roll and he was pissed, and rightfully so. He wanted to finish his turn. The Box Man looked at Jimmy and said he was getting too loud. Swear to God! In a major Nevada casino the house was complaining about noise. Usually they want it loud, the louder the better. But not here and not now. They were trying to cool us down and throw a damper on the game.

The other guy refused to take the dice. God bless him! Then they were passed to the guy after him. He also refused. And so it went, all the way around the table, until they got back to Jimmy. Once again the Box Man would not give the dice to Jimmy. We had a stalemate. For several minutes play came to a halt. I looked down and decided to count my chips. I had nearly $4,000 in front of me. I had started with $100. Mataya and Varner were sitting on a good fifteen thousand each. All in all, we had beaten the Sands for at least sixty grand in an hour or so. I found out later that a full refill on the dice table was $50,000. We had made them refill once already, and then put a big dent in their new stack.

They wanted out! They wanted to close the table. It had become a losing proposition for the Sands. They couldn't win here. If the dice got cold we would all quit anyway. And if the dice stayed hot we could beat them for many thousands more. Remember, we were all betting high now, even me. I gathered up my chips and headed for the cage. Without a word being spoken, one player after another did likewise, and followed me to the cage. The game was over. We had beaten the house!

MAKING MOVIES

Away from the world of pool tournaments and poolrooms, I also managed to get involved on the periphery of Hollywood. I was occasionally hired to shoot a few shots for television shows or low budget films. The pay was good, *scale* for a Technical Advisor being over $400 a day. One day I got a call from someone at Touchstone Productions, inquiring if I was available to coach some actors working on a pool scene. Of course, I replied. I'd be glad to help out. I was told to come out to the studio for an interview with Barrie Osborne, the producer of the film.

I cruised out to Burbank the next day, not having a clue what the film was about, or who Barrie Osborne was for that matter. I got ushered to the set and into the production offices. A secretary informed me that Barrie was in a meeting with Warren and would be back shortly. Warren who, I asked? Why Warren Beatty of course, she said. Now I know this is a big deal if Warren Beatty is involved. Turns out he was the star and the director.

Soon Mr. Osborne returns and greets me warmly in his office. We chat a little about pool in general and my background in the game. Then we talk about money and how much I expect to be paid. I told him *scale* would be fine with me. After he's satisfied, he says he'd like me to meet Warren. Well okay, why not. Let's say hi to Warren. Barrie takes me over to the make-up trailer. We go inside, and Warren Beatty is in a chair having his make-up applied. He has a big apron around his neck, and the make-up lady is doing her thing. Barrie tells Warren that he wants him to meet me, possibly the new technical advisor for the pool scene. Warren signals the lady to stop, and he turns in the chair and eyes me up and down. "Howya doin," he says. "I'm doin just fine," I reply. "Good, welcome aboard." And just like that, I'm hired to work on *Dick Tracy*!

I go back with Barrie to the production offices, and they go over details like *call sheets, call times, shooting days,* and the like. Someone hands me a script with the poolroom scene outlined in red. I am told to read it over and report back tomorrow at 9 AM to go to work. I will be paid $440 a day. Not too shabby in 1989 dollars.

The next day I drive back out to the Burbank Studios, on top of the world. I am now working on a major motion picture with Warren Beatty. I am led to a large sound stage (a building the size of an airplane hanger), and inside is a small room made up to look like a police station *day room* from the 1930's. The *day room* was a place for cops to hang out, relax and maybe grab a quick bite to eat. In this make believe *day room* there is an antique style pool table. The pool scene will consist of one game of Eight Ball between The Kid and Tess. And the actors playing the parts are Charlie Korsmo (The Kid) and Sean Young (Tess). That morning I meet both of them. And that's it, I'm done for the day. They just wanted me to see the set and meet the actors. I had been there less than two hours.

I'm feeling a little disappointed on my way back to the production office. I only earned two hours pay today. So I ask the girl, as I sign out, how the hourly pay is figured. She looks at me like I'm crazy. "You aren't paid by the hour. If you are on the call sheet, you get paid for the entire day whether you work one hour or eight. You just have to show up on time and be ready if we need you. You can go home now. You're done for the day." Sweet! It's only 11 AM and I had earned my day's pay. I think I'm gonna like this job.

From that day on when I was called to the set, I had to practice with Charlie or Sean, and teach them how to shoot the pool shots that I'd created for them. Many of the guys on the film crew would come by the day room and see how our practice was going. The conversation always seemed to revolve around pool players they knew, or how good they used to play. It seemed like most of them wanted to challenge me to a game. As much as possible I accommodated them, as time allowed. Two or three guys prodded me about gambling, and joked about making a bet with me. I knew that if I took advantage of this situation, it may be my last day on the job. I wouldn't take that risk for a few dollars. My first responsibility was teaching the actors their shots, and making them look like pool players. That's what they were paying me for, not to hustle the crew.

Charlie was a very bright young man and enthusiastic about playing pool. He had a major role in the movie as did Sean Young. She was long, lean and beautiful, with a good head on her shoulders. We had many great conversations about all kinds of things. One funny story she told me had to do with her part in the movie *Baby*, about a baby dinosaur. Sean was not a big star who was immediately recognizable, so she tended to blend in wherever she went. She was more of a *character* actor.

Anyway, a few days after *Baby* had been released, Sean was eating lunch somewhere and overheard a conversation on a nearby table about the movie. The people were discussing the various actors who starred in it, and they weren't sure who played her part. A lady at the table said she thought it might have been Sean Young in that role, but a man with her said no it wasn't. He said it was someone else. Sean hears this and leans over to the man and says, "It WAS Sean Young." "How do you know?" he asks her. She replies, "I am Sean Young!" He looks at her a moment and shakes his head, "No, that wasn't you in that part." Yes, some people are really that dumb!

So we practice together for a week, and I get to know Sean and Charlie pretty well. The next day we are supposed to shot the pool scene, two full pages in the script. Then disaster strikes. Sean is canned off the movie. She has some kind of run in with Warren and it's all over. He fires her. Rumors are swirling all over the set, but I'll leave those tales for the gossip columns. I'll stick to the facts as I know them. I am told by the production people not to come back in until I'm called. A day or two goes by and I get called to come in the next day. Dutifully I show up and they tell me to report back to the pool set. Waiting for me there is Glenne Headley, the new Tess. I must start all over, teaching her the same shots. All good though, it means I am on the job for one more week.

Finally the big day comes and the little day room is overrun with production people. When I get there cameras and equipment are everywhere, and there must be thirty people hustling all around getting things prepared for the *shoot*. I stay in the background, content to observe all the goings on. I just hope Charlie and Glenne can make the shots I taught them. The magic moment finally arrives and Warren is summoned to the set.

You have to remember that I had only met Warren Beatty for a moment. He did acknowledge me if he saw me on the set, nodding his head as he walked by, but that's about the extent of our contact. Now he enters the day room, readied now for the filming, and looks all around at how things are set up. I am standing in the background, off to one side. Warren looks right at me and exclaims, "Jay, how do you think we should shoot this scene?" What, huh, you talking to me? I was breathless for a moment but quickly regained my composure, "Well Warren, I've never shot a movie before, but I've worked on a lot of TV shows." He nods his head in recognition of television, the small screen I think they call it. I realize I need to continue. "I think the camera should be here, where the player is shooting directly at it." Warren motions for the camera to be moved.

The rest of the day I work side by side with Warren Beatty. We do at least ten to twelve *takes* of each shot, and then we have to decide which ones look the best. There may have been only three or four successful shots, so that narrows the choices. Warren would ask me at the end of each series, which *take* I thought was the best. I made sure to remember the ones where the actor made the shot. I would pick out a couple I thought looked the best and tell Warren, "number three or number six." Warren would turn to his cameraman and say, "Save number three and number six." Hey, I was co-director for a day!

So that's how the day went, Warren Beatty and Jay Helfert; moviemakers, buddies, partners....Well, I can dream can't I? Sad to say, he's never called me again for any of his movies. Believe me I was ready!

The punch line to this story is that I told everyone about my big day working with Warren Beatty. I was also invited to be at the premiere for *Dick Tracy*. I was so proud of my little pool scene in the movie. I couldn't wait to see it on the *big* screen. I got there early and my name was on the guest list. I'm a big shot now. I sat smugly in the immense theater, enjoying "my movie". Only one small problem. There was no pool scene! Damn and double damn! What happened to my big scene? My career was ruined! I was a has been before I even got started.

Outside the theater I spot Barrie Osborne. He gives me a friendly hello. So I ask him point blank, "Barrie, what happened to the pool scene?" He can see the obvious disappointment on my face. "Jay, the movie was too long, well over two hours. We had to cut some of it, and the pool scene got the ax." My bubble had been burst. I was beyond consolation. In poker terms, this was a really bad beat.

LEAVE 'EM LAUGHING

The following two stories are a couple of the funniest things I can remember from my years running tournaments.

In the first scenario a vintage Earl Strickland is playing a young Shannon Daulton in Reno in the early 90's. The match is tied at 3-3 when Earl goes on one on his patented runs. In mere minutes he strings together six racks. It looks like Shannon won't even come back to the table as Earl breaks in rack number thirteen, leading 9-3. In fact, poor Shannon is sitting in his chair with a dazed expression on his face. Earl has literally shot him into a coma.

Earl makes a ball on the break and runs down to the five ball, which rests inches away from the side pocket. Position on the six is tricky, and Earl chooses to use inside english and spin the cue ball along the side rail, off the end rail and back up the table along the same side. He uses a little too much english, and the cue ball hugs the side rail and slides into the corner pocket. Earl has scratched and Shannon has ball in hand.

At first Shannon appears to not realize what has happened. When he sees that there is no cue ball on the table, it dawns on him that it's his turn. Slowly he rises from his chair, uncertain what to do. He moves awkwardly to the table, and stands motionless for a minute. It is painfully obvious that Shannon is lost in space somewhere. He now removes the five ball from the side pocket, and places it on the table in the approximate location where it was before Earl's last shot. What's up with this we are all wondering? It's getting more interesting by the moment. No one says a word, not even Earl. Everyone is watching carefully now to see what Shannon will do next.

Shannon next retrieves the cue ball from the corner pocket. He holds it for a few seconds and then places it in position to make the five ball. He has given himself ball in hand on the five ball, that he has mistakenly placed back on the table. Now the audience is starting to crack up. People are stifling their laughter, and smirks and little bits of noise are being heard. Shannon stops a moment, and looks around the room. He still doesn't know what's going on. He may realize something is wrong, but he doesn't get the joke yet. Finally, out of mercy, Earl stands and takes his cue and taps the cue ball. He tells Shannon that he has ball in hand on the six ball, not the five, and he scoops the five back into the side pocket.

Suddenly it dawns on Shannon. He wakes up! He's embarrassed, and begins to laugh at himself. The crowd erupts in laughter, never having seen anything quite like this before. It isn't often that we get to see a famous pool player forget how to play pool. But we just did!

The second little embarrassing moment came at the Resorts tournament I was working with Billy Staton ("Weenie Beenie"), the promoter, and Pat Fleming, my co-director. At the players meeting there had been a long discussion about what constitutes an illegal push shot. Billy had gotten very involved in that discussion, much to the dismay of Pat Fleming and myself. Billy was a great promoter, but we didn't want him out there calling hits or making rulings.

Sure enough in one of the matches a shot came up where the cue ball was a fraction of an inch from the object ball, and the player wanted to know if he could shoot straight through it. Both Pat and I came down, and a discussion ensued about what he could and could not do on this particular shot. Before we could get it resolved, Billy came over and picked up the player's cue off the table. Pat and I looked at each other like what's going on here. Billy proceeds to launch into a dissertation about the rules pertaining to a shot like this. Okay so far.

Then he announces, "This is what you can't do." Billy gets down and fires the cue ball right through the object ball. Balls fly everywhere, the entire table has been rearranged. Billy stands back up, proud of himself for showing us the foul. Pat and I stand by horrified at first, and then we start to laugh. We can't help ourselves. The two players are not as amused, and begin to argue about what to do next. Only then does Billy realize what he's done. He tries to cover up saying, "Oh I didn't realize this was a match in progress." Everyone who witnessed this is now convulsing in laughter. They can't help themselves either, it's that funny.

We finally resolved this one by re-racking the balls and letting the same guy break again. And Billy has to agree not to make any more calls.

IN CONCLUSION

The last player who I backed successfully was Tang Hoa. Back in the 90's, he was playing great pool and was anxious to get out there and play in all the big events. He just lacked the funds to do so. I told him I would stake him in any tournament he wanted to play in. Our deal was I would pay all his expenses, and would get that money back "off the top". The first money he won would go towards repaying me for the expenses. Any additional prize money after that, we would split 50-50.

Tang did well, winning over $40,000 our first year together, with expenses of about $10,000. This was the first year of the Camel Pro Tour, a series of eight tournaments each having a $75,000 purse. There was an additional $300,000 bonus fund paid to the top twenty players at the end of the tour. The Camel Tour looked very promising for the pro players, and R.J. Reynolds (who owned the Camel brand) was prepared to increase the scope of the Camel Tour in future years. Bigger purses, more events and more money for everyone was on the horizon.

Once again the players shot themselves in the foot. They bickered and complained about how Camel was running things, and kept making more and more demands. The MPBA commissioner Don Mackey was after Camel for money too, perhaps a little perturbed that he wasn't sharing in the largesse. He was being left out in the cold by Camel and he didn't like it. He wanted his piece of the pie, so he instigated the players to bite the hand that was feeding them. Mackey's favorite technique was to hold all day marathon meetings, where he would pound his philosophy into their heads. In essence, he brainwashed them.

The final straw for Camel may have been at the tournament in Milwaukee where Earl was playing Corey Deuel in the finals. Earl became upset with the way Scott Smith was racking the balls and abruptly quit in the middle of the match. He walked out in the finals in front of a crowded room full of spectators. A major embarrassment for Camel. It may have been the final nail in the coffin that sealed the fate of the Camel Pro Tour.

The following year a lawsuit was brought by Mackey against R.J. Reynolds, and the ownership of the tour was turned over to the MPBA. The players were not paid for the final five events of the year ($375,000), with Mackey promising to make good after the lawsuit was settled. The players hung on for one reason only. There still remained a $300,000 Bonus fund to be awarded at the end of the year, that was guaranteed by Camel. The players competed in the final five events for zero prize money, just to earn points toward the bonus money. To this day they have not received the prize money for those five tournaments. What happened to that money, and all the other receipts from those tournaments, is a question that remains unanswered. I have my own opinion.

Mackey also put together World Team Billiards, a series of competitions between teams from different countries. These matches were televised, but once again the players were paid in IOU's. Mackey distributed "stock" in World Team Billiards to the players, which turned out to be worthless. In the end a settlement was reached with R.J. Reynolds and several hundred thousand was paid to the MPBA. None of that money ever reached the player/stockholders either. Where it went I can only imagine. Mackey sold these guys a bill of goods telling them what they wanted to hear. He told them he would make them rich and famous. In hindsight it looks like only one person made any money off his association with men's pro pool. And it wasn't a player.

Tang and I continued our partnership for a couple more years, and he made it to the finals of the 1998 U.S. Open. His opponent was Buddy Hall, and they would play one Race To Eleven for the $25,000 first prize. Second prize was $12,500. There was also some calcutta money on the line, $6,000 for first and $4,000 for second. Tang and I talked it over, and we were prepared to make a deal with Buddy to *save* a little of the prize money. We decided that a $2,500 saver would be good, making first now $22,500 and second $15,000. I just had to talk to Buddy and see if he would agree to this.

Buddy saw me first, standing outside the practice room. He motioned for me to come over and have a chat with him. He asked me if Tang wanted to do a saver. I told him that was fine with us, what did he have in mind? He said, "How about $4,000?" "Okay, but I have to talk to Tang first," I told him. I walked back in the practice room, winked at Tang and walked back out. We had a deal. Buddy won the match and we got $16,500 for second, plus half the calcutta money. Someone else had bought Tang in the calcutta, and I bought half from him.

The best part was when we went in the office to see Barry Behrman, the promoter of the Open. He had piles of money stacked on his desk. Barry counted out the 16.5K first and the 2K next. Tang and I walked out $18,500 to the good.

On that high note I will bring this treatise to an end. There are more stories about the pool world I can share with you on some future occasion, but for now these will have to suffice. Thank you for indulging me.

At the Final Table, 2005 World Series of Poker, Limit Hold'em.
I finished fifth for $42,000!

THANK YOU

I hoped you liked my stories and gained a new appreciation for some of the players of yesteryear. It was a truly golden era for pool in America and I feel fortunate to have been a witness to so much of it.

On my website jayhelfert.com you will find some memorabilia from events I worked on in years past. I invite you to check it out and drop me a line at my e-mail address. Take care and good shooting.

Jay Helfert

My Pool Mentor, UJ Puckett.